Amish Cooking

pil

Publications International, Ltd.

Favorite Brand Name Recipes at www.fbnr.com

Pictured on the back cover *(top to bottom):* Toffee Bread Pudding with Cinnamon Toffee Sauce *(page 168)* and Homestyle Skillet Chicken *(page 30).*

Cover illustrated by Amy Flynn.

Interior illustrations by Roberta Polfus.

ISBN-13: 978-1-4127-2059-5
ISBN-10: 1-4127-2059-1

Library of Congress Control Number: 2004109276

Manufactured in China.

8 7 6 5 4 3 2 1

Microwave Cooking: Microwave ovens vary in wattage. Use the cooking times as guidelines and check for doneness before adding more time.

Preparation/Cooking Times: Preparation times are based on the approximate amount of time required to assemble the recipe before cooking, baking, chilling or serving. These times include preparation steps such as measuring, chopping and mixing. The fact that some preparations and cooking can be done simultaneously is taken into account. Preparation of optional ingredients and serving suggestions is not included.

Contents

Meat and Poultry

Herbed Chicken & Vegetables

>   2 medium all-purpose potatoes, thinly sliced (about
>   1 pound)
>   2 medium carrots, sliced
>   4 bone-in chicken pieces (about 2 pounds)
>   1 envelope LIPTON® RECIPE SECRETS® Savory Herb
>   with Garlic Soup Mix
>   ¹/₃ cup water
>   1 tablespoon BERTOLLI® Olive Oil

1. Preheat oven to 425°F. In broiler pan without the rack, place potatoes and carrots; arrange chicken on top. Pour soup mix blended with water and oil over chicken and vegetables.

2. Bake uncovered 40 minutes or until chicken is thoroughly cooked, juices run clear and vegetables are tender.   *Makes 4 servings*

Prep Time: *10 minutes*
Cook Time: *40 minutes*

Herbed Chicken & Vegetables

Roasted Turkey Breast with Cherry & Apple Rice Stuffing

3³/₄ cups water
3 boxes UNCLE BEN'S® Long Grain & Wild Rice
    Butter & Herb Fast Cook Recipe
¹/₂ cup butter or margarine, divided
¹/₂ cup dried red tart cherries
1 large apple, peeled and chopped (about 1 cup)
¹/₂ cup sliced almonds, toasted*
1 bone-in turkey breast (5 to 6 pounds)

*To toast almonds, place them on a baking sheet. Bake 10 to 12 minutes in a preheated 325°F oven or until they are golden brown, stirring occasionally.

1. In large saucepan, combine water, rice, contents of seasoning packets, 3 tablespoons butter and cherries. Bring to a boil. Cover; reduce heat to low and simmer 25 minutes or until all water is absorbed. Stir in apple and almonds; set aside.

2. Preheat oven to 325°F. Place turkey breast, skin side down, on rack in roasting pan. Loosely fill breast cavity with rice stuffing. (Place any remaining stuffing in greased baking dish; cover and refrigerate. Bake alongside turkey for 35 to 40 minutes or until heated through.)

3. Place sheet of heavy-duty foil over stuffing, molding it slightly over sides of turkey. Carefully invert turkey, skin side up, on rack. Melt remaining 5 tablespoons butter; brush some of butter over surface of turkey.

4. Roast turkey, uncovered, 1 hour; baste with melted butter. Continue roasting 1¹/₄ to 1³/₄ hours, basting occasionally with melted butter, until meat thermometer inserted into center of thickest part of turkey breast, not touching bone, registers 170°F. Let turkey stand, covered, 15 minutes before carving.   *Makes 6 to 8 servings*

Roasted Turkey Breast with Cherry & Apple Rice Stuffing

Buttermilk Oven-Fried Chicken

1½ **cups buttermilk**
4 **teaspoons garlic powder, divided**
2 **teaspoons salt**
2 **teaspoons dried thyme leaves, divided**
1 **teaspoon dried sage**
1 **teaspoon paprika**
½ **teaspoon black pepper**
2½ **pounds chicken pieces, skin removed**
Nonstick cooking spray
1½ **cups dry bread crumbs**
¼ **cup all-purpose flour**

1. Whisk buttermilk, 3 teaspoons garlic powder, salt, 1 teaspoon thyme, sage, paprika and pepper in large bowl until well blended. Add chicken; turn to coat. Cover and refrigerate at least 5 hours or overnight.

2. Preheat oven to 400°F. Line 2 baking sheets with foil; spray with cooking spray.

3. Combine bread crumbs, flour, remaining 1 teaspoon garlic powder and 1 teaspoon thyme in large shallow bowl. Remove chicken from buttermilk mixture, allowing excess to drip off. Coat chicken pieces one at a time with crumb mixture. Shake off excess crumbs. Place on prepared baking sheets; let stand 10 minutes.

4. Spray top portions of chicken with cooking spray. Bake about 50 minutes or until chicken is golden brown and juices run clear, turning once and spraying with additional cooking spray halfway through baking time.   *Makes about 8 servings*

Buttermilk Oven-Fried Chicken

Chili Meatloaf and Potato Bake

1¹/₂ **pounds ground turkey**
³/₄ **cup salsa**
1 **tablespoon chili powder**
1 **egg, beaten**
1¹/₃ **cups French's® French Fried Onions, divided**
¹/₂ **teaspoon salt**
¹/₄ **teaspoon ground black pepper**
2 **cups prepared hot mashed potatoes**
2 **cups (8 ounces) shredded taco blend cheese, divided**

1. *Preheat oven to 375°F. Combine ground turkey, salsa, chili powder, egg, ²/₃ cup French Fried Onions, salt and pepper until blended. Press turkey mixture into 9-inch square baking dish.*

2. *Bake 25 minutes or until turkey is cooked through and juices run clear. Drain off fat.*

3. *Combine potatoes and 1 cup cheese. Spread evenly over meatloaf. Sprinkle with remaining cheese and onions; bake 5 minutes or until cheese is melted and onions are golden.*   *Makes 6 servings*

Tip: *Prepare instant mashed potatoes for 4 servings.*

Variation: *For added Cheddar flavor, substitute* **French's**® *Cheddar French Fried Onions for the original flavor.*

Prep Time: *15 minutes*
Cook Time: *30 minutes*

Chili Meatloaf and Potato Bake

Maple-Mustard Pork Chops

    2 tablespoons maple syrup, divided
    1 tablespoon olive oil
    2 teaspoons whole-grain mustard
    2 center-cut pork loin chops (6 ounces each)
      Nonstick cooking spray
 $^1/_3$ cup water

1. Preheat oven to 375°F. Combine maple syrup, olive oil and mustard in small bowl. Brush syrup mixture over both sides of pork chops.

2. Spray medium ovenproof skillet with cooking spray; heat skillet over medium-high heat. Add chops; brown on both sides. Add water; cover and bake 20 to 30 minutes or until barely pink in centers.   *Makes 2 servings*

Kielbasa and Sauerkraut Skillet Dinner

    2 tablespoons olive oil
    1 pound kielbasa sausage, cut in $^1/_4$-inch-thick slices
    1 small red onion, thinly sliced
    1 small green bell pepper, cored, seeded and thinly
      sliced
    2 cups sauerkraut, rinsed and well drained
    2 teaspoons Dijon mustard
 $^1/_2$ teaspoon caraway seeds
 $^1/_4$ teaspoon salt
 $^1/_4$ teaspoon black pepper

1. Heat oil in large skillet. Add kielbasa, onion and bell pepper. Cook over medium heat 5 to 10 minutes or until vegetables are tender and sausage is lightly browned, stirring occasionally. Drain fat, if desired.

2. Add sauerkraut, mustard, caraway seeds, salt and black pepper to skillet. Cook over medium heat 3 to 5 minutes or until heated through.

Makes 4 servings

Maple-Mustard Pork Chop

Roast Chicken with Peppers

1 chicken (3 to 3¹/₂ pounds), cut into pieces
3 tablespoons olive oil, divided
1 tablespoon plus 1¹/₂ teaspoons chopped fresh
    rosemary or 1¹/₂ teaspoons dried rosemary
1 tablespoon fresh lemon juice
1¹/₄ teaspoons salt, divided
³/₄ teaspoon freshly ground black pepper, divided
3 bell peppers (preferably 1 red, 1 yellow and
    1 green)
1 medium onion

1. Preheat oven to 375°F. Rinse chicken in cold water; pat dry with paper towels. Place in shallow roasting pan.

2. Combine 2 tablespoons oil, rosemary and lemon juice; brush over chicken. Sprinkle 1 teaspoon salt and ¹/₂ teaspoon pepper over chicken. Roast 15 minutes.

3. Cut bell peppers lengthwise into ¹/₂-inch-thick strips. Cut onion into thin wedges. Toss vegetables with remaining 1 tablespoon oil, ¹/₄ teaspoon salt and ¹/₄ teaspoon pepper. Spoon vegetables around chicken; roast about 40 minutes or until vegetables are tender and chicken is no longer pink and juices run clear. Serve chicken with vegetables and pan juices.

Makes 6 servings

Roast Chicken with Peppers

Sauerbraten

     3 large onions, sliced
     8 tablespoons Butter Flavor CRISCO® Stick or
         8 tablespoons Butter Flavor CRISCO® Shortening,
         divided
     3 cups cider vinegar
     1 cup packed dark brown sugar
    20 whole cloves
    10 peppercorns
     6 bay leaves
    10 gingersnap cookies, crushed
     3 cups water, divided
     1 (4- to 6-pound) beef rump roast
    $^1/_2$ cup sour cream
    $^1/_2$ cup golden raisins

Cook onions in 2 tablespoons CRISCO® Shortening until golden brown. Carefully add vinegar, brown sugar, cloves, peppercorns, bay leaves and cookie crumbs. Bring to a boil. Add 1 cup water; remove from heat and cool mixture to room temperature.

Place rump roast and cooled marinade in smallest possible container. Cover with plastic wrap. Marinate in refrigerator for 3 days, turning meat 1 to 2 times per day. Remove roast from container; reserve marinade. Pat roast dry with paper towel.

Preheat oven to 350°F.

Melt 6 tablespoons CRISCO® Shortening in a large skillet; brown roast on all sides. Place in roasting pan and roast, uncovered, for about 2$^1/_2$ hours or until internal temperature reaches 165°F. Let meat rest 20 minutes before carving.

Meanwhile, bring marinade to a boil. Boil until reduced by half; strain. Stir in sour cream and golden raisins. Serve sauce with carved roast.

Makes 6 to 8 servings

Sauerbraten

Ham Loaf

1 pound ground pork
1/2 pound ham, ground
3/4 cup milk
1/2 cup fresh bread crumbs
1 egg
1 tablespoon instant tapioca
1/2 teaspoon prepared horseradish
3 to 4 drops red food color (optional)

Sauce
1/2 cup ketchup
2 tablespoons packed brown sugar
1 tablespoon Worcestershire sauce

In large bowl, mix together pork, ham, milk, crumbs, egg, tapioca, horseradish and food color, if desired, until well blended. Place mixture in loaf pan and bake at 325°F for 1 hour. In small bowl, stir together Sauce ingredients. Pour Sauce over Ham Loaf and bake for another 30 minutes, basting occasionally with Sauce. Remove from oven; let stand 10 minutes before removing from pan. Slice to serve.   *Makes 6 servings*

Prep Time: *10 minutes*
Cook Time: *90 minutes*

Favorite recipe from **National Pork Board**

Tip: To make fresh bread crumbs, first remove the crusts from two slices of bread. Tear bread into small pieces. Day-old firm-textured bread works best.

Cheesy Ham and Macaroni

1 (1.8 ounce) package white sauce mix
2 cups milk
$^1/_2$ cup grated Parmesan cheese
$^1/_2$ cup cubed American cheese
$^1/_8$ teaspoon ground black pepper
7 ounces macaroni, cooked according to package
   directions, drained
1$^1/_2$ cups diced fully cooked ham
1 cup frozen green peas, thawed

In a large saucepan, stir together white sauce mix and milk.* Following package directions, cook until thickened. Stir in cheeses and pepper. Add macaroni, ham and peas; cook, stirring until heated through. Serve hot.

Makes 6 servings

*If you want to make a white sauce from scratch, melt 3 tablespoons butter in a saucepan. Stir in $^1/_4$ cup flour and cook until mixture bubbles. Stir in 2 cups milk and cook, stirring, until thickened.

Favorite recipe from **National Pork Board**

Country Chicken Stew with Dumplings

        1 **tablespoon BERTOLLI® Olive Oil**
        1 **chicken (3 to 3¹/₂ pounds), cut into serving pieces**
            (with or without skin)
        4 **large carrots, cut into 2-inch pieces**
        3 **ribs celery, cut into 1-inch pieces**
        1 **large onion, cut into 1-inch wedges**
        1 **envelope LIPTON® RECIPE SECRETS® Savory Herb**
            with Garlic Soup Mix*
    1¹/₂ **cups water**
     ¹/₂ **cup apple juice**
        Parsley Dumplings (optional, recipe follows)

Also terrific with LIPTON® RECIPE SECRETS® Golden Onion Soup Mix.

In 6-quart Dutch oven or heavy saucepot, heat oil over medium-high heat and brown ¹/₂ of the chicken; remove and set aside. Repeat with remaining chicken. Return chicken to Dutch oven. Stir in carrots, celery, onion and savory herb with garlic soup mix blended with water and apple juice. Bring to a boil over high heat. Reduce heat to low; simmer covered 25 minutes or until chicken is thoroughly cooked, juices run clear and vegetables are tender.

Meanwhile, prepare Parsley Dumplings. Drop 12 rounded tablespoonfuls of batter into simmering broth around chicken. Continue simmering covered 10 minutes or until toothpick inserted in center of dumplings comes out clean. Season stew, if desired, with salt and pepper.

Makes about 6 servings

Parsley Dumplings: In medium bowl, combine 1¹/₃ cups all-purpose flour, 2 teaspoons baking powder, 1 tablespoon chopped fresh parsley and ¹/₂ teaspoon salt; set aside. In measuring cup, blend ²/₃ cup milk, 2 tablespoons melted butter or margarine and 1 egg. Stir milk mixture into flour mixture just until blended.

Variation: Add 1 pound quartered red potatoes to stew with carrots; eliminate dumplings.

Menu Suggestion: Serve this as a meal-in-one!

Country Chicken Stew with Dumplings

Family-Style Creamy Chicken and Noodles

8 ounces uncooked yolk-free wide egg noodles
4 cups water
1 pound boneless skinless chicken breasts
1½ cups chopped onions
¾ cup chopped celery
½ teaspoon salt
½ teaspoon dried thyme leaves
1 bay leaf
⅛ teaspoon white pepper
1 can (10-ounce) condensed reduced-sodium cream of chicken soup, undiluted
½ cup nonfat buttermilk

1. Cook pasta according to package directions, omitting salt. Drain; set aside.

2. Meanwhile, bring water to a boil in Dutch oven over high heat. Add chicken breasts, onions, celery, salt, thyme, bay leaf and pepper. Return to a boil. Reduce heat to low; simmer, uncovered, 35 minutes. Remove chicken. Cut into ½-inch pieces; set aside.

3. Increase heat to high. Return liquid in Dutch oven to a boil. Continue cooking until liquid and vegetables have reduced to 1 cup. Remove from heat; discard bay leaf. Whisk in soup and buttermilk until well blended. Add chicken pieces and pasta; toss to blend. Sprinkle with parsley, if desired.

Makes 4 servings

Family-Style Creamy Chicken and Noodles

Wild Rice Meatball Primavera

1 **pound ground turkey**
$^1/_2$ **cup seasoned bread crumbs**
1 **egg, beaten**
2 **tablespoons oil**
1 **can (10$^3/_4$ ounces) condensed cream of mushroom
   soup, undiluted**
2 **cups water**
1 **package (16 ounces) frozen broccoli medley, thawed**
1 **box UNCLE BEN'S® Long Grain & Wild Rice Fast
   Cook Recipe**

1. *Combine turkey, bread crumbs and egg; mix well. Shape into 1$^1/_4$- to 1$^1/_2$-inch meatballs (about 20 to 22 meatballs).*

2. *Heat oil in large skillet over medium-high heat until hot. Cook meatballs 6 to 7 minutes or until brown on all sides. Drain on paper towels.*

3. *Combine soup and water in skillet; bring to a boil. Add meatballs, vegetables and contents of seasoning packet, reserving rice. Cover; reduce heat and simmer 5 minutes, stirring occasionally.*

4. *Add reserved rice to skillet; mix well. Cover; cook 5 minutes more or until hot. Remove from heat; stir well. Cover and let stand 5 minutes before serving.*   *Makes 6 servings*

Wild Rice Meatball Primavera

Baked Barbecue Chicken

1 (3-pound) broiler-fryer, cut up
1 small onion, cut into slices
1¹/₂ cups ketchup
¹/₂ cup firmly packed light brown sugar
¹/₄ cup Worcestershire sauce
2 tablespoons lemon juice
1 tablespoon liquid smoke

Preheat oven to 375°F. Spray 13×9-inch baking dish with nonstick cooking spray. Place chicken in prepared dish; top with onion slices.

Combine ketchup, brown sugar, Worcestershire sauce, lemon juice and liquid smoke in small saucepan. Heat over medium heat 2 to 3 minutes or until sugar dissolves. Pour over chicken.

Bake chicken 1 hour or until juices run clear. Discard onion slices. Let stand 10 minutes before serving.   *Makes 6 servings*

Serving Suggestion: Serve with baked potatoes, crusty French bread and a tossed green salad.

Tip: Liquid smoke is a commercial product produced by infusing a liquid with smoke. Brush it on broiled meat or poultry to give it a grilled flavor or add it to sauces, marinades and other dishes like this.

Baked Barbecue Chicken

Italian-Style Brisket

1 cup fat-free reduced-sodium beef broth or water, divided
$^1/_2$ cup chopped onion
1 clove garlic, minced
1 can (14$^1/_2$ ounces) no-salted-added diced tomatoes, undrained
$^3/_4$ teaspoon dried oregano leaves
$^1/_4$ teaspoon dried thyme leaves
$^1/_4$ teaspoon black pepper
1 small well-trimmed beef brisket (about 1$^1/_4$ pounds)
3 cups sliced mushrooms
3 cups halved and thinly sliced zucchini (about 1 pound)
3 cups cooked egg noodles

1. Heat $^1/_4$ cup beef broth in Dutch oven. Add onion and garlic; cover and simmer 5 minutes.

2. Stir in tomatoes with juice, remaining $^3/_4$ cup beef broth, oregano, thyme and pepper. Bring to a boil. Reduce heat to low; add beef brisket. Cover and simmer 1$^1/_2$ hours, basting occasionally with tomato mixture.

3. Add mushrooms and zucchini; simmer, covered, 30 to 45 minutes or until beef is tender.

4. Remove beef. Simmer vegetable mixture 5 to 10 minutes to thicken slightly. Cut beef across the grain into thin slices. Serve beef with vegetable sauce and noodles.

Makes 6 servings

Italian-Style Brisket

Homestyle Skillet Chicken

      1 tablespoon Cajun seasoning blend
    1/2 teaspoon plus 1/8 teaspoon black pepper, divided
    1/2 teaspoon salt, divided
      4 chicken thighs
      2 tablespoons vegetable oil
      4 cloves garlic, minced
    3/4 pound small red or new potatoes (about 8),
          quartered
     12 pearl onions, peeled*
      1 cup peeled baby carrots
      2 ribs celery, halved lengthwise and sliced diagonally
          into 1/2-inch pieces
    1/2 red bell pepper, diced
      2 tablespoons all-purpose flour
   1 1/2 cups canned reduced-sodium chicken broth
      2 tablespoons finely chopped fresh parsley

*To peel pearl onions, drop in boiling water for 30 seconds and plunge immediately into ice water. The peel should slide right off.

1. Combine Cajun seasoning, 1/2 teaspoon pepper and 1/4 teaspoon salt in small bowl. Rub mixture on all sides of chicken.

2. Heat oil in large heavy skillet over medium-high heat. Add garlic and chicken; cook until chicken is browned, about 3 minutes per side. Transfer chicken to plate; set aside.

3. Add potatoes, onions, carrots, celery and bell pepper to skillet. Cook and stir 3 minutes. Sprinkle flour over vegetables; stir to coat. Slowly stir in chicken broth, scraping up browned bits from bottom of skillet. Bring mixture to a boil, stirring constantly.

4. Reduce heat to medium-low. Return chicken to skillet. Cover and cook about 30 minutes or until juices of chicken run clear. Increase heat to medium-high; cook, uncovered, about 5 minutes or until sauce is thickened. Season with remaining 1/4 teaspoon salt and 1/8 teaspoon pepper. Sprinkle with parsley before serving.   *Makes 4 servings*

Homestyle Skillet Chicken

Baked Ham with Apple-Raspberry Sauce

    1 (3-pound) canned ham
    1 cup chopped green apples
   ¹/₂ cup SMUCKER'S® Red Raspberry Preserves
   ¹/₂ cup SMUCKER'S® Apple Jelly
   ³/₄ cup apple cider
    1 tablespoon cider vinegar
    2 tablespoons cornstarch
       Endive or parsley sprigs
       Whole crabapples

Bake ham according to package directions.

Mix chopped apples, SMUCKER'S® preserves and jelly in medium saucepan. Combine cider, vinegar and cornstarch; stir into saucepan. Heat to boiling; boil, stirring constantly, until thickened, about 1 minute.

Slice ham and arrange on platter; garnish with endive and crabapples. Serve with sauce. *Makes 8 to 10 servings*

Note: Fresh crabapples are too sour to eat out of hand, but the canned spiced varieties are delicious with pork and poultry.

Ranch Crispy Chicken

   ¹/₄ cup unseasoned dry bread crumbs or cornflake
        crumbs
    1 packet (1 ounce) HIDDEN VALLEY® The Original
        Ranch® Salad Dressing & Seasoning Mix
    6 bone-in chicken pieces

Combine bread crumbs and salad dressing & seasoning mix in a gallon-size Glad® Zipper Storage Bag. Add chicken pieces; seal bag. Shake to coat chicken. Bake chicken on ungreased baking pan at 375°F for 50 minutes or until no longer pink in center and juices run clear. *Makes 4 to 6 servings*

Baked Ham with Apple-Raspberry Sauce

Quick & Easy Broccoli Chicken

1 (6.9-ounce) package RICE-A-RONI® Chicken Flavor
2 tablespoons margarine or butter
1 teaspoon dried basil
4 boneless, skinless chicken breast halves (about
   1 pound)
2 cups broccoli flowerets
1 tomato, chopped
1 cup (4 ounces) shredded mozzarella or Cheddar
   cheese

1. In large skillet over medium heat, sauté rice-vermicelli mix with margarine until vermicelli is golden brown.

2. Slowly stir in 2 cups water, basil and Special Seasonings. Bring to a boil. Place chicken over rice. Reduce heat to low. Cover; simmer 10 minutes.

3. Stir in broccoli and tomato. Cover; simmer 10 minutes or until rice is tender and chicken is no longer pink inside. Sprinkle with cheese. Cover; let stand 3 minutes or until cheese is melted.   *Makes 4 servings*

Tip: If you prefer, use green beans or whole-kernel corn instead of broccoli.

Prep Time: 5 minutes
Cook Time: 30 minutes

Meat Loaf

Vegetable cooking spray
$^1/_2$ **cup catsup**
$^1/_4$ **cup brown sugar**
 2 **teaspoons dry mustard**
 1 **pound ground beef**
$^1/_2$ **cup bread crumbs**
$^1/_4$ **cup MRS. DASH® Onion & Herb Blend**
 2 **eggs**

Preheat oven to 350°F. Spray 8×4 inch loaf pan with vegetable cooking spray. Combine catsup, brown sugar and mustard in small bowl; mix well. Set aside. Combine ground beef, bread crumbs, Onion & Herb Blend, eggs and half of catsup sauce in large bowl; mix well. Pat into prepared loaf pan. Bake 40 minutes. Spread remaining sauce over meat. Return to oven and cook additional 10 minutes. Let stand 5 minutes before serving.

Makes 6 servings

Prep Time: *10 minutes*
Cook Time: *55 minutes*

Roast Garlic Chicken

1 **whole broiler/fryer chicken (about 3 to 4 pounds)**
2 **tablespoons lemon juice**
1½ **teaspoons LAWRY'S® Garlic Powder With Parsley**
2 **teaspoons LAWRY'S® Seasoned Salt**

Sprinkle chicken with lemon juice, Garlic Powder With Parsley and Seasoned Salt over outside and inside cavity of chicken. Spray 13×9×2-inch baking dish and roasting rack with nonstick cooking spray. Place chicken, breast side up, on roasting rack. Roast in 400°F oven until meat is no longer pink and juices run clear when cut (175° to 180°F at thickest joint), about 60 to 70 minutes. Let stand 10 minutes before carving.

Makes 6 servings

Hint: Loosely 'crunch up' some foil in the dish around the chicken to keep grease from splattering in the oven.

Prep Time: 10 minutes
Cook Time: 60 to 70 minutes

Roast Garlic Chicken

Pork Schnitzel

1½ pounds center cut pork loin cut into six 4-ounce
   portions approximately ½-inch thick
2 eggs, beaten
1 cup all-purpose flour
2½ cups bread crumbs
1 teaspoon salt
½ teaspoon pepper
¼ teaspoon ground nutmeg
½ cup or ½ stick Butter Flavor Crisco® Shortening

Place pork, one piece at a time, in gallon-size plastic bag and pound, starting in center of meat and working out, until very thin. Place the pounded pieces between waxed paper and refrigerate.

Meanwhile, in a baking dish place the flour; in another beat 2 eggs and in a third baking dish mix bread crumbs, salt, pepper and nutmeg. Arrange pans in order of use: flour, eggs, then bread crumbs.

Melt Butter Flavor CRISCO® in a heavy skillet until very hot (about 325°F). Bread each piece of pork by first dredging in flour (shake off any excess), then egg and bread crumbs, pressing crumbs onto meat. Fry 1 or 2 pieces at a time, about 2 minutes per side. Drain on paper towels and serve.

Makes 6 servings

Serving Suggestion: *Pork Schnitzel is great served with a squeeze of lemon and capers!*

Beef Tips and Egg Noodles

  2 **packages (0.88 ounce each) LAWRY'S® Brown Gravy**
     Mix
  1 **can (6 ounces) tomato paste**
  $^1/_2$ **teaspoon LAWRY'S® Seasoned Salt**
  2 **tablespoons vegetable or olive oil**
$1^1/_2$ **pounds boneless beef top sirloin or beef sirloin tip,**
     cut into $^1/_2$-inch cubes
  $^1/_4$ **cup chopped green bell pepper**
  8 **ounces wide egg noodles, cooked**

In medium bowl, whisk together Brown Gravy Mix, 2 cups water, tomato paste and Seasoned Salt until smooth; set aside. In large skillet, heat oil over high heat. Add beef and and bell pepper; cook until beef is browned, about 5 minutes. Stir in gravy mixture. Bring to a boil; reduce heat to low, cover and cook 8 minutes, stirring occasionally. Serve over hot egg noodles.

Makes 4 to 6 servings

Meal Idea: Add 1 package (8 ounces) sliced fresh mushrooms or 1 can (4 ounces) sliced mushrooms; cook with gravy and peppers for extra flavor.

Hint: Sirloin is recommended because less tender cuts of beef need longer cooking times.

Prep Time: *10 to 12 minutes*
Cook Time: *35 to 40 minutes*

Casseroles

Pork with Savory Apple Stuffing

    1 *package (6 ounces) corn bread stuffing mix*
    1 *can (14$\frac{1}{2}$ ounces) chicken broth*
    1 *small apple, peeled, cored and chopped*
  $\frac{1}{4}$ *cup chopped celery*
1$\frac{1}{3}$ *cups French's® French Fried Onions, divided*
    4 *boneless pork chops, $\frac{3}{4}$ inch thick (about 1 pound)*
  $\frac{1}{2}$ *cup peach-apricot sweet & sour sauce*
    1 *tablespoon French's® Honey Dijon Mustard*

1. *Preheat oven to 375°F. Combine stuffing mix, broth, apple, celery and $\frac{2}{3}$ cup French Fried Onions in large bowl. Spoon into bottom of greased shallow 2-quart baking dish. Arrange chops on top of stuffing.*

2. *Combine sweet & sour sauce with mustard in small bowl. Pour over pork. Bake 40 minutes or until pork is no longer pink in center.*

3. *Sprinkle with remaining onions. Bake 5 minutes or until onions are golden.*   *Makes 4 servings*

Prep Time: *10 minutes*
Cook Time: *45 minutes*

Pork with Savory Apple Stuffing

Chicken, Asparagus & Mushroom Bake

1 tablespoon butter
1 tablespoon olive oil
2 boneless skinless chicken breasts (about $^1/_2$ pound),
    cut into bite-size pieces
2 cloves garlic, minced
1 cup sliced mushrooms
2 cups sliced asparagus
    Black pepper
1 package (about 6 ounces) corn bread stuffing mix
$^1/_4$ cup dry white wine (optional)
1 can (14$^1/_2$ ounces) fat-free reduced-sodium chicken
    broth
1 can (10$^1/_2$ ounces) condensed low-sodium cream of
    asparagus or cream of chicken soup, undiluted

1. Preheat oven to 350°F. Heat butter and oil in large skillet until butter is melted. Cook and stir chicken and garlic about 3 minutes over medium-high heat until chicken is no longer pink. Add mushrooms; cook and stir 2 minutes. Add asparagus; cook and stir about 5 minutes or until asparagus is crisp-tender. Season with pepper.

2. Transfer mixture to 2$^1/_2$-quart casserole or 6 small casseroles. Top with stuffing mix.

3. Add wine to skillet, if desired; cook and stir 1 minute over medium-high heat, scraping up any browned bits from bottom of skillet. Add broth and soup; cook and stir until well blended.

4. Pour broth mixture into casserole; mix well. Bake, uncovered, about 35 minutes (30 minutes for small casseroles) or until heated through and lightly browned.   *Makes 6 servings*

Chicken, Asparagus & Mushroom Bake

Potato Sausage Casserole

1 pound bulk pork sausage or ground pork
1 can (10$\frac{3}{4}$ ounces) condensed cream of mushroom
    soup, undiluted
$\frac{3}{4}$ cup milk
$\frac{1}{2}$ cup chopped onion
$\frac{1}{2}$ teaspoon salt
$\frac{1}{4}$ teaspoon black pepper
3 cups sliced potatoes
$\frac{1}{2}$ tablespoon butter, cut into small pieces
1$\frac{1}{2}$ cups (6 ounces) shredded Cheddar cheese

1. Preheat oven to 350°F. Spray 1$\frac{1}{2}$-quart casserole with nonstick cooking spray; set aside.

2. Cook sausage in large skillet over medium-high heat, stirring to separate, until no longer pink; drain fat.

3. Stir together soup, milk, onion, salt and pepper in medium bowl.

4. Place half of potatoes in prepared casserole. Top with half of soup mixture; top with half of sausage. Repeat layers, ending with sausage. Dot with butter.

5. Cover pan with foil. Bake 1$\frac{1}{4}$ to 1$\frac{1}{2}$ hours or until potatoes are tender. Uncover; sprinkle with cheese. Return to oven; bake until cheese is melted and bubbly.

Makes 6 servings

Potato Sausage Casserole

Spicy Chicken Casserole with Corn Bread

2 tablespoons olive oil
4 boneless skinless chicken breasts, cut into bite-size
  pieces
1 envelope (about 1 ounce) taco seasoning
1 can (about 15 ounces) black beans, rinsed and
  drained
1 can (14$\frac{1}{2}$ ounces) diced tomatoes, drained
1 can (about 10 ounces) Mexican-style corn, drained
1 can (about 4 ounces) diced chilies, drained
$\frac{1}{2}$ cup mild salsa
1 box (about 8$\frac{1}{2}$ ounces) corn bread mix, plus
  ingredients to prepare
$\frac{1}{2}$ cup (2 ounces) shredded Cheddar cheese
$\frac{1}{4}$ cup chopped red bell pepper

1. *Preheat oven to 350°F. Spray 2-quart casserole with nonstick cooking spray. Set aside. Heat oil in large skillet over medium heat. Cook chicken until no longer pink.*

2. *Sprinkle taco seasoning over chicken. Add black beans, tomatoes, corn, chilies and salsa; stir until well mixed. Transfer to prepared dish.*

3. *Prepare corn bread mix according to package directions, adding cheese and bell pepper. Spread batter over chicken mixture.*

4. *Bake 30 minutes or until corn bread is golden brown.*

Makes 4 to 6 servings

Spicy Chicken Casserole with Corn Bread

Classic Macaroni and Cheese

2 **cups elbow macaroni**
3 **tablespoons butter or margarine**
$^1/_4$ **cup chopped onion (optional)**
2 **tablespoons all-purpose flour**
$^1/_2$ **teaspoon salt**
$^1/_8$ **teaspoon pepper**
2 **cups milk**
2 **cups (8 ounces) SARGENTO® Chef Style or Fancy Mild Cheddar Shredded Cheese, divided**

Cook macaroni according to package directions; drain. In medium saucepan, melt butter and, if desired, cook onion about 5 minutes or until tender. Stir in flour, salt and pepper. Gradually add milk and cook, stirring occasionally, until thickened. Remove from heat. Add 1$^1/_2$ cups cheese and stir until cheese melts. Combine cheese sauce with cooked macaroni. Place in 1$^1/_2$-quart casserole; top with remaining $^1/_2$ cup cheese. Bake at 350°F 30 minutes or until bubbly and cheese is golden brown.

Makes 6 servings

Tip: For a smooth cheese sauce, remove the sauce mixture from the heat and stir in the shredded cheese until it is completely melted.

Chicken Rice Casserole

2 tablespoons MRS. DASH® Minced Onion Medley
2 cups 2% milk
¼ cup butter
2 tablespoons all-purpose flour
1 can (7 ounces) sliced mushrooms, drained or 1 cup sliced fresh mushrooms
¼ cup chopped fresh parsley
3 cups cooked rice
2 cups cubed cooked chicken or turkey
½ cup diced cooked ham
2 cups coarsely chopped cooked broccoli

Preheat oven to 350°F. Combine Mrs. Dash Minced Onion Medley and milk in a small saucepan or 2-cup glass microwavable measuring cup. Heat just until warm. Melt butter in a large nonstick skillet over medium heat. Whisk in flour. Gradually whisk in milk mixture and heat until thickened; whisk constantly. Remove from heat and stir in mushrooms and parsley. Spray a square glass 2-quart baking dish with nonstick coating spray. Layer rice, chicken, ham and broccoli in prepared dish. Pour sauce evenly over layered ingredients. Bake at 350°F for 25 to 30 minutes or until heated thoroughly.

Makes 8 servings

Prep Time: 10 minutes
Cook Time: 30 minutes

Chicken Pot Pie with Onion Biscuits

1 package (1.8 ounces) classic white sauce mix
2³/₄ cups milk, divided
¹/₄ teaspoon dried thyme leaves
1 package (10 ounces) frozen peas and carrots, thawed
1 package (10 ounces) roasted carved chicken breast, cut into bite-size pieces
1 cup all-purpose baking mix
1¹/₃ cups French's® French Fried Onions, divided
¹/₂ cup (2 ounces) shredded Cheddar cheese

1. Preheat oven to 400°F. Prepare white sauce mix according to package directions with 2¹/₄ cups milk; stir in thyme. Mix vegetables, chicken and prepared white sauce in shallow 2-quart casserole.

2. Combine baking mix, ²/₃ cup French Fried Onions and remaining ¹/₂ cup milk in medium bowl until blended. Drop 6 to 8 spoonfuls of dough over chicken mixture.

3. Bake 25 minutes or until biscuits are golden. Sprinkle biscuits with cheese and remaining onions. Bake 3 minutes or until cheese is melted and onions are golden.   *Makes 6 servings*

Tip: You may substitute 2 cups cut-up cooked chicken for the roasted, carved chicken breast.

Variation: For added Cheddar flavor, substitute **French's® Cheddar French Fried Onions** for the original flavor.

Prep Time: 15 minutes
Cook Time: 33 minutes

Chicken Pot Pie with Onion Biscuits

Turkey Tetrazzini Casserole

6 ounces egg noodles
2 HERB-OX® chicken flavored instant low sodium
   bouillon packets
1 (15-ounce) can evaporated skim milk
¼ cup all-purpose flour
⅛ teaspoon ground nutmeg
2 cups diced cooked turkey
6 green onions, sliced
1 (2-ounce) jar chopped pimientos
¼ cup grated Parmesan cheese, divided
2 tablespoons slivered almonds, toasted

Preheat oven to 350°F. Cook egg noodles as package directs. Meanwhile, in large saucepan, over medium-high heat, bring bouillon, evaporated milk, flour and nutmeg to a boil. Cook, stirring until thick and bubbly about 2 minutes. Add turkey, cooked noodles, green onions, pimientos and 2 tablespoons Parmesan cheese. Transfer turkey mixture to a lightly greased 2-quart casserole dish. Sprinkle with remaining cheese and almonds. Bake 20 to 25 minutes or until hot and bubbly.

Makes 6 servings

Prep Time: 20 minutes
Total Time: 45 minutes

Hot Dogs with Potatoes and Kraut

$^1\!/_4$ cup butter
2 large apples, cored and cut into $^1\!/_4$-inch rings
$3^1\!/_2$ cups undrained sauerkraut
2 cups dairy sour cream
$^1\!/_3$ cup grated Parmesan cheese
$^1\!/_3$ cup fine dry bread crumbs
1 teaspoon salt
3 medium potatoes, cooked and cut into $^1\!/_3$-inch slices
1 pound HILLSHIRE FARM® Hot Dogs, halved lengthwise and crosswise

Melt butter in large skillet. Arrange apple rings in skillet and cook over medium heat about 8 minutes, turning apple rings once. Remove apple rings. Add sauerkraut to butter in skillet; mix well. Combine sour cream, cheese, crumbs and salt; mix well. Make a layer of half each of the potatoes, sauerkraut, apple rings, Hot Dogs and sour cream mixture in buttered $2^1\!/_2$-quart casserole. Repeat layer of potatoes, sauerkraut, apple rings and Hot Dogs. Dot top of casserole with remaining sour cream mixture. Bake in 325°F oven for 30 minutes or until sour cream mixture is lightly browned.   *Makes 4 to 6 servings*

Beef Stroganoff Casserole

1 pound lean ground beef
1/4 teaspoon salt
1/8 teaspoon black pepper
1 teaspoon vegetable oil
8 ounces sliced mushrooms
1 large onion, chopped
3 cloves garlic, minced
1/4 cup beef broth
1 can (10 3/4 ounces) condensed cream of mushroom
   soup, undiluted
1/2 cup sour cream
1 tablespoon Dijon mustard
4 cups cooked egg noodles
Chopped fresh parsley (optional)

1. Preheat oven to 350°F. Spray 13×9-inch baking dish with nonstick cooking spray.

2. Place beef in large skillet; season with salt and pepper. Brown beef over medium-high heat until no longer pink, stirring to separate meat. Drain fat from skillet; set aside.

3. Heat oil in same skillet over medium-high heat until hot. Add mushrooms, onion and garlic; cook and stir 2 minutes or until onion is tender. Add broth. Reduce heat to medium-low and simmer 3 minutes. Remove from heat; stir in soup, sour cream and mustard until well blended. Return beef to skillet.

4. Place noodles in prepared dish. Pour beef mixture over noodles; stir until noodles are well coated. Bake, uncovered, 30 minutes or until heated through. Sprinkle with parsley, if desired.   *Makes 6 servings*

Beef Stroganoff Casserole

Turkey and Stuffing Bake

1 jar (4½ ounces) sliced mushrooms
¼ cup butter or margarine
½ cup diced celery
½ cup chopped onion
1¼ cups HIDDEN VALLEY® The Original Ranch®
    Dressing, divided
⅔ cup water
3 cups seasoned stuffing mix
⅓ cup sweetened dried cranberries
3 cups coarsely shredded cooked turkey (about
    1 pound)

Drain mushrooms, reserving liquid; set aside. Melt butter over medium-high heat in a large skillet. Add celery and onion; sauté for 4 minutes or until soft. Remove from heat and stir in ½ cup dressing, water and reserved mushroom liquid. Stir in stuffing mix and cranberries until thoroughly moistened. Combine turkey, mushrooms and remaining ¾ cup dressing in a separate bowl; spread evenly in a greased 8-inch baking dish. Top with stuffing mixture. Bake at 350°F for 40 minutes or until bubbly and brown.   *Makes 4 to 6 servings*

Turkey and Stuffing Bake

Spicy Pork Chop Casserole

Nonstick cooking spray
2 cups frozen corn
2 cups frozen diced hash brown potatoes
1 can (14^1/$_2$ ounces) diced tomatoes with basil, garlic, and oregano, drained
2 teaspoons chili powder
1 teaspoon dried oregano leaves
^{1}/$_2$ teaspoon ground cumin
^{1}/$_8$ teaspoon crushed red pepper
1 teaspoon olive oil
4 (3-ounce) boneless pork loin chops, cut about ^{3}/$_4$ inch thick
^{1}/$_4$ teaspoon black pepper
^{1}/$_4$ cup (1 ounce) shredded reduced-fat Monterey Jack cheese (optional)

1. Preheat oven to 375°F.

2. Lightly spray nonstick skillet with cooking spray. Add corn; cook and stir over medium-high heat about 5 minutes or until corn begins to brown. Add potatoes; cook and stir about 5 minutes more or until potatoes begin to brown. Add tomatoes, chili powder, oregano, cumin and red pepper; stir until well blended.

3. Lightly spray 8×8×2-inch baking dish with cooking spray. Transfer corn mixture to prepared dish.

4. Wipe skillet with paper towel. Add oil and pork chops to skillet. Cook pork chops over medium-high heat until brown on one side. Remove pork chops; place, browned side up, on top of corn mixture in baking dish. Sprinkle with pepper. Bake, uncovered, 20 minutes or until meat is juicy and barely pink in center. Sprinkle with cheese, if desired. Let stand 2 to 3 minutes.

Makes 4 servings

Prep Time: 15 minutes
Bake Time: 20 minutes

Spicy Pork Chop Casserole

Chicken Divan Casserole

1 cup uncooked rice
1 cup coarsely shredded carrots*
   Nonstick cooking spray
4 boneless skinless chicken breasts
2 tablespoons butter or margarine
3 tablespoons all-purpose flour
1/4 teaspoon salt
   Black pepper
1 cup fat-free chicken broth
3/4 cup milk or half-and-half
1/3 cup plus 2 tablespoons grated Parmesan cheese,
   divided
1 pound frozen broccoli florets

Coarsely shredded carrots are available in the produce sections of many large supermarkets or shred them on a hand-held grater.

1. Preheat oven to 350°F. Lightly grease 12×8-inch baking dish.

2. Prepare rice according to package directions. Stir in carrots. Spread mixture into prepared baking dish.

3. Spray large skillet with cooking spray. Heat over medium-high heat. Brown chicken breasts about 2 minutes on each side. Arrange over rice.

4. To prepare sauce, melt butter in 2-quart saucepan over medium heat. Whisk in flour, salt and pepper to taste; cook and stir 1 minute. Gradually whisk in broth and milk. Cook and stir until mixture comes to a boil. Reduce heat; simmer 2 minutes. Remove from heat. Stir in 1/3 cup cheese.

5. Arrange broccoli around chicken. Pour sauce over chicken and broccoli. Sprinkle remaining 2 tablespoons cheese over chicken.

6. Cover with foil; bake 30 minutes. Remove foil; bake 10 to 15 minutes or until chicken is no longer pink in center and broccoli is hot.

Makes 6 servings

Chicken Divan Casserole

Oven-Baked Stew

2 pounds boneless beef chuck or round steak, cut
    into 1-inch cubes
¼ cup all-purpose flour
1⅓ cups sliced carrots
1 can (14 to 16 ounces) whole peeled tomatoes,
    undrained and chopped
1 envelope LIPTON® RECIPE SECRETS® Onion
    Soup Mix*
½ cup dry red wine or water
1 cup fresh or canned sliced mushrooms
1 package (8 ounces) medium or broad egg noodles,
    cooked and drained

*Also terrific with LIPTON® RECIPE SECRETS® Beefy Onion, Onion Mushroom or Beefy Mushroom
Soup Mix.*

1. Preheat oven to 425°F. In 2½-quart shallow casserole, toss beef with
flour, then bake uncovered 20 minutes, stirring once.

2. Reduce heat to 350°F. Stir in carrots, tomatoes, soup mix and wine.

3. Bake covered 1½ hours or until beef is tender. Stir in mushrooms and
bake covered an additional 10 minutes. Serve over hot noodles.

Makes 8 servings

Prep Time: *20 minutes*
Cook Time: *2 hours*

Oven-Baked Stew

Lit'l Smokies 'n' Macaroni 'n' Cheese

1 package (7¹/₄ ounces) macaroni and cheese mix,
    prepared according to package directions
1 pound HILLSHIRE FARM® Lit'l Smokies
1 can (10³/₄ ounces) condensed cream of celery or
    mushroom soup, undiluted
¹/₃ cup milk
1 tablespoon minced parsley (optional)
1 cup (4 ounces) shredded Cheddar cheese

Preheat oven to 350°F.

Combine prepared macaroni and cheese, Lit'l Smokies, soup, milk and parsley, if desired, in medium bowl. Pour into small greased casserole. Sprinkle Cheddar cheese over top. Bake, uncovered, 20 minutes or until heated through.

Makes 8 servings

Ham Pot Pie

1 (10³/₄-ounce) can condensed cream of broccoli soup,
    undiluted
¹/₃ cup milk
¹/₈ teaspoon dried thyme leaves
¹/₄ teaspoon coarsely ground pepper
2 (5-ounce) cans HORMEL® chunk ham, drained and
    flaked*
1 (10-ounce) package frozen vegetables, thawed and
    drained.
1 (4¹/₂-ounce) can refrigerated buttermilk biscuits
    (6 count)

*HORMEL® chunk breast of chicken may be substituted here.

Heat oven to 400°F. In 1¹/₂-quart round baking dish, combine soup, milk, thyme and pepper. Stir in ham and vegetables. Bake 20 to 25 minutes. Separate biscuits; cut each biscuit into quarters. Arrange biscuits over ham mixture. Bake 12 to 15 minutes longer or until biscuits are golden brown.

Makes 6 servings

Lit'l Smokies 'n' Macaroni 'n' Cheese

Soups and Salads

Cheddar Broccoli Soup

1 tablespoon olive oil
1 rib celery, chopped (about $^1/_2$ cup)
1 carrot, chopped (about $^1/_2$ cup)
1 small onion, chopped (about $^1/_2$ cup)
$^1/_2$ teaspoon dried thyme leaves, crushed (optional)
2 cans (13$^3/_4$ ounces each) chicken broth
1 jar (1 pound) RAGÚ® Cheese Creations!® Double
    Cheddar Sauce
1 box (10 ounces) frozen chopped broccoli, thawed
    and drained

In 3-quart saucepan, heat olive oil over medium heat and cook celery, carrot, onion and thyme 3 minutes or until vegetables are almost tender. Add chicken broth and bring to a boil over high heat. Reduce heat to medium and simmer, uncovered, 10 minutes.

In food processor or blender, purée vegetable mixture until smooth; return to saucepan. Stir in Ragú Cheese Creations! Double Cheddar Sauce and broccoli. Cook 10 minutes or until heated through.

Makes 6 (1-cup) servings

Cheddar Broccoli Soup

Country Chicken Chowder

1 pound chicken tenders
2 tablespoons butter or margarine
1 small onion, chopped
1 rib celery, sliced
1 small carrot, sliced
1 can (10¾ ounces) condensed cream of potato soup,
   undiluted
1 cup milk
1 cup frozen corn
½ teaspoon dried dill weed

1. Cut chicken tenders into ½-inch pieces.

2. Melt butter in large saucepan or Dutch oven over medium-high heat. Add chicken; cook and stir 5 minutes.

3. Add onion, celery and carrot; cook and stir 3 minutes. Stir in soup, milk, corn and dill; reduce heat to low. Cook about 8 minutes or until corn is tender and chowder is heated through. Add salt and pepper to taste.

Makes 4 servings

Tip: For a special touch, garnish soup with croutons and fresh dill. For a hearty winter meal, serve the chowder in hollowed-out toasted French rolls or small round sourdough loaves.

Prep and Cook Time: *27 minutes*

Country Chicken Chowder

Refreshing Turkey Salad

3 cups cooked rice, cooled to room temperature
2 cups diced cantaloupe
1½ cups cooked turkey breast cubes
¼ cup packed mint leaves
¼ cup packed parsley
1 clove garlic, halved
1 container (8 ounces) plain nonfat yogurt
Lettuce leaves
Assorted fresh fruit for garnish (optional)

Combine rice, cantaloupe and turkey in large bowl. Finely chop mint, parsley and garlic in food processor. Add yogurt and blend. Add to rice mixture; toss lightly. Cover and chill 2 hours. Serve on lettuce leaves. Garnish with fresh fruit, if desired.   *Makes 4 servings*

Favorite recipe from **USA Rice Federation**

Chunky Potato Bacon Soup

1 package (32 ounces) frozen Southern-style hash brown potatoes, thawed
1 quart milk
1 can (10¾ ounces) condensed cream of celery soup
1 cup (6 ounces) cubed processed cheese
⅓ cup cooked chopped bacon (4 slices uncooked)
1 tablespoon French's® Worcestershire Sauce
1⅓ cups French's® French Fried Onions

1. Combine potatoes, milk, soup, cheese, bacon and Worcestershire in large saucepot. Heat to boiling over medium-high heat, stirring often.

2. Heat French Fried Onions in microwave on HIGH 2 minutes or until golden. Ladle soup into bowls. Sprinkle with onions. Garnish with fresh minced parsley if desired.   *Makes 6 servings*

Prep Time: 5 minutes
Cook Time: 10 minutes

Refreshing Turkey Salad

Country Bean Soup

1¼ cups dried navy beans or lima beans, rinsed and
     drained
  4 ounces salt pork or fully cooked ham, chopped
¼ cup chopped onion
½ teaspoon dried oregano leaves
¼ teaspoon salt
¼ teaspoon ground ginger
¼ teaspoon dried sage
¼ teaspoon black pepper
  2 cups fat-free (skim) milk
  2 tablespoons butter

1. Place navy beans in large saucepan; add enough water to cover beans. Bring to a boil; reduce heat and simmer 2 minutes. Remove from heat; cover and let stand for 1 hour. (Or, cover beans with water and soak overnight.)

2. Drain beans and return to saucepan. Stir in 2½ cups water, salt pork, onion, oregano, salt, ginger, sage and pepper. Bring to a boil; reduce heat. Cover and simmer 2 to 2½ hours or until beans are tender. (If necessary, add more water during cooking.) Add milk and butter, stirring until mixture is heated through and butter is melted. Season with additional salt and pepper, if desired.

Makes 6 servings

Country Bean Soup

Sensational Seven Layer Rice Salad

1 (7.2-ounce) package RICE-A-RONI® Rice Pilaf
2 tablespoons margarine or butter
1 (15-ounce) can black beans, drained and rinsed
1 cup ranch dressing
1 cup sour cream
4 cups fresh spinach leaves or romaine lettuce, cut
   into thin strips
3 medium tomatoes, chopped
2 cups (8 ounces) shredded Cheddar cheese
1 small red onion, halved and thinly sliced
½ pound bacon, crisply cooked, drained and chopped
3 radishes, sliced (optional)
  Tomato wedges (optional)

1. In large skillet over medium heat, sauté rice-pasta mix with margarine until pasta is golden brown.

2. Slowly add 1¾ cups water and Special Seasonings; bring to a boil. Reduce heat to low. Cover; simmer 17 to 22 minutes or until rice is tender.

3. Stir in black beans. Spread mixture in 13×9-inch baking pan. Cool completely; set aside.

4. In small bowl, mix ranch dressing and sour cream; set aside.

5. In large clear glass bowl, layer spinach, tomatoes, cheese, rice-bean mixture and onion, pressing gently after each layer. Spread dressing mixture over top of salad. Sprinkle with bacon. Garnish with radishes and tomato, if desired.   *Makes 8 servings*

Prep Time: *30 minutes*
Cook Time: *25 minutes*

Sensational Seven Layer Rice Salad

Pork and Cabbage Soup

$^1/_2$ **pound pork loin, cut into** $^1/_2$**-inch cubes**
1 **medium onion, chopped**
2 **strips bacon, finely chopped**
2 **cups canned beef broth**
2 **cups canned chicken broth**
1 **can (28 ounces) tomatoes, cut-up and drained**
2 **medium carrots, sliced**
$^3/_4$ **teaspoon dried marjoram leaves**
1 **bay leaf**
$^1/_8$ **teaspoon black pepper**
$^1/_4$ **medium cabbage, chopped**
2 **tablespoons chopped fresh parsley**
Additional chopped fresh parsley

1. Cook and stir pork, onion and bacon in 5-quart Dutch oven over medium heat until meat loses its pink color and onion is slightly tender. Remove from heat. Drain fat.

2. Stir in beef and chicken broth. Stir in tomatoes, carrots, marjoram, bay leaf and pepper. Bring to a boil over high heat. Reduce heat to medium-low; simmer, uncovered, about 30 minutes. Remove and discard bay leaf. Skim off fat.

3. Stir cabbage into soup. Bring to a boil over high heat. Reduce heat to medium-low; simmer, uncovered, about 15 minutes or until cabbage is tender.

4. Remove soup from heat; stir in 2 tablespoons parsley. Ladle into bowls. Garnish each serving with additional parsley.   *Makes 6 servings*

German Potato Salad

    4 cups sliced peeled Colorado potatoes
    4 slices bacon
  $^3/_4$ cup chopped onion
  $^1/_4$ cup sugar
    3 tablespoons all-purpose flour
$1^1/_2$ teaspoons salt
    1 teaspoon celery seeds
  $^1/_4$ teaspoon black pepper
    1 cup water
  $^3/_4$ cup vinegar
    2 hard-cooked eggs, chopped

Cook potatoes in boiling water until tender; drain. Meanwhile, cook bacon in medium skillet until crisp. Drain on paper towels; cool and crumble. Cook and stir onion in drippings until tender. Combine sugar, flour, salt, celery seeds and pepper; blend in water and vinegar. Stir into onion in skillet; heat until bubbly. Pour over combined potatoes, bacon and eggs; toss. Serve immediately.
Makes 6 servings

Favorite recipe from **Colorado Potato Administrative Committee**

Inside-Out Egg Salad

    6 hard-cooked eggs, peeled
  $^1/_3$ cup mayonnaise
  $^1/_4$ cup chopped celery
    1 tablespoon French's® Classic Yellow® Mustard

1. Cut eggs in half lengthwise. Remove egg yolks. Combine yolks, mayonnaise, celery and mustard in small bowl. Add salt and pepper to taste.

2. Spoon egg yolk mixture into egg whites. Sprinkle with paprika, if desired. Chill before serving.
Makes 12 servings

Prep Time: *20 minutes*

Veg•All® Italian Soup

2 tablespoons butter
1 cup diced onion
1 cup shredded cabbage
2 cups water
2 cans (14$\frac{1}{2}$ ounces each) stewed tomatoes
1 can (15 ounces) VEG•ALL® Original Mixed
   Vegetables, drained
1 tablespoon chopped fresh parsley
$\frac{1}{2}$ teaspoon dried basil
$\frac{1}{2}$ teaspoon dried oregano
$\frac{1}{2}$ teaspoon black pepper

In large saucepan, melt butter. Stir in onion and cabbage. Heat for
2 minutes. Add water; cover and simmer for 10 minutes. Stir in tomatoes,
Veg•All and seasonings. Simmer for 10 minutes.   *Makes 6 servings*

Easy Chicken Salad

$\frac{1}{4}$ cup reduced-fat mayonnaise
$\frac{1}{4}$ cup finely diced celery
2 tablespoons sweet pickle relish
1 tablespoon minced onion
$\frac{1}{2}$ teaspoon Dijon mustard
$\frac{1}{8}$ teaspoon salt
   Black pepper
2 cups cubed cooked chicken
   Salad greens

1. Combine mayonnaise, celery, relish, onion, mustard, salt and pepper in
medium bowl; mix well. Stir in chicken. Cover and refrigerate at least
1 hour.

2. Serve on salad greens with fruit, if desired.   *Makes 2 servings*

Veg•All® Italian Soup

Parsley, Ham and Pasta Salad

        2 cups uncooked elbow macaroni
        2 cups (12 ounces) CURE 81® ham, cut into strips
        1 cup sliced celery
      1/2 cup sliced green onions
        1 cup mayonnaise or salad dressing
        1 cup packed fresh parsley, finely chopped
      1/4 cup grated Parmesan cheese
      1/4 cup white wine vinegar
        1 clove garlic, minced

Cook macaroni according to package directions. In large bowl, combine
ham, macaroni, celery and green onions. In small bowl, combine
mayonnaise, parsley, cheese, vinegar and garlic; toss with pasta. Cover and
refrigerate 1 to 2 hours to blend flavors.   *Makes 6 to 8 servings*

Cheeseburger Soup

      1/2 pound ground beef
     31/2 cups water
      1/2 cup cherry tomato halves or chopped tomato
        1 pouch LIPTON® Soup Secrets Ring-O-Noodle Soup
             Mix with Real Chicken Broth
        1 cup (4 ounces) Cheddar cheese, shredded

Shape ground beef into 16 mini burgers.

In large saucepan, thoroughly brown burgers; drain. Add water, tomatoes
and soup mix; bring to a boil. Reduce heat and simmer uncovered, stirring
occasionally, 5 minutes or until burgers are cooked and noodles are tender.
Stir in cheese.   *Makes about 4 (1-cup) servings*

Parsley, Ham and Pasta Salad

Corn and Tomato Chowder

1¹/₂ **cups peeled, diced plum tomatoes**
 ³/₄ **teaspoon salt, divided**
  2 **ears corn, husks removed**
  1 **tablespoon margarine**
 ¹/₂ **cup finely chopped shallots**
  1 **clove garlic, minced**
  1 **can (12 ounces) evaporated skimmed milk**
  1 **cup chicken broth**
  1 **tablespoon finely chopped fresh sage or 1 teaspoon
    rubbed sage**
 ¹/₄ **teaspoon black pepper**
  1 **tablespoon cornstarch**
  2 **tablespoons cold water**

1. Place tomatoes in nonmetal colander over bowl. Sprinkle with ¹/₂ teaspoon salt; toss to mix well. Allow tomatoes to drain at least 1 hour.

2. Meanwhile, cut corn kernels off cobs into small bowl. Scrape cobs with dull side of knife blade to extract liquid from cobs into same bowl; set aside. Discard 1 cob; break remaining cob in half.

3. Heat margarine in heavy medium saucepan over medium-high heat until melted and bubbly. Add shallots and garlic; reduce heat to low. Cover and cook about 5 minutes or until shallots are soft and translucent. Add evaporated milk, broth, sage, pepper and reserved corn cob halves. Bring to a boil over high heat. Reduce heat to low; simmer, uncovered, 10 minutes. Remove and discard cob halves.

4. Add corn with liquid; return to a boil over medium-high heat. Reduce heat to low; simmer, uncovered, 15 minutes more. Dissolve cornstarch in water; add to chowder, mixing well. Stir until thickened. Remove from heat; stir in drained tomatoes and remaining ¹/₄ teaspoon salt. Spoon into bowls. Garnish with additional fresh sage, if desired.   *Makes 4 servings*

Corn and Tomato Chowder

Tuna Pasta Primavera Salad

2 cups cooked and chilled small shell pasta
1½ cups halved cherry tomatoes
½ cup thinly sliced carrots
½ cup sliced celery
½ cup chopped seeded peeled cucumber
½ cup thinly sliced radishes
½ cup thawed frozen peas
¼ cup slivered red bell pepper
2 tablespoons minced green onion, including tops
1 (7-ounce) pouch of STARKIST® Premium Albacore
   or Chunk Light Tuna
1 cup salad dressing of choice
Bibb or red leaf lettuce
Fresh herbs, for garnish

In large bowl, combine all ingredients except lettuce and herbs. Chill several hours. If using oil and vinegar dressing, stir salad mixture occasionally to evenly marinate ingredients. Place lettuce leaves on each plate; spoon salad over lettuce. Garnish with fresh herbs, if desired.

Makes 6 servings

Prep Time: *25 minutes*

Tuna Pasta Primavera Salad

Spinach, Bacon and Mushroom Salad

1 large bunch (12 ounces) fresh spinach leaves,
   washed, drained and torn
³/₄ cup sliced fresh mushrooms
4 slices bacon, crisply cooked and crumbled
³/₄ cup croutons
4 hard-cooked eggs, finely chopped
   Black pepper, to taste
³/₄ cup prepared HIDDEN VALLEY® The Original
   Ranch® Dressing

In medium salad bowl, combine spinach, mushrooms and bacon; toss. Top
with croutons and eggs; season with pepper. Pour salad dressing over all.

Makes 6 servings

Colorful Turkey Pasta Salad

2¹/₂ cups tri-colored rotini pasta, cooked and drained
2 cups cubed cooked turkey, white meat preferred
¹/₂ cup thinly sliced green onions
¹/₄ cup chopped celery
¹/₄ cup chopped fresh parsley
1¹/₂ teaspoons chopped fresh tarragon or ¹/₂ teaspoon
   dried tarragon leaves
2 tablespoons reduced-calorie mayonnaise
2 tablespoons tarragon vinegar
1 tablespoon fresh lemon juice
1 tablespoon canola or olive oil

1. In large bowl, combine pasta, turkey, onions, celery, parsley and
tarragon.

2. In small bowl, mix together mayonnaise, vinegar, lemon juice and oil.
Add to turkey mixture.

3. Mix well, coating all surfaces. Cover and refrigerate 1 to 2 hours or until
chilled throughout. *Makes 4 servings*

Favorite recipe from **California Poultry Federation**

Spinach, Bacon and Mushroom Salad

Ground Beef, Spinach and Barley Soup

12 ounces 95% lean ground beef
4 cups water
1 can (14$\frac{1}{2}$ ounces) no-salt-added stewed tomatoes, undrained
1$\frac{1}{2}$ cups thinly sliced carrots
1 cup chopped onion
$\frac{1}{2}$ cup quick-cooking barley
1$\frac{1}{2}$ teaspoons beef bouillon granules
1$\frac{1}{2}$ teaspoons dried thyme leaves
1 teaspoon dried oregano leaves
$\frac{1}{2}$ teaspoon garlic powder
$\frac{1}{4}$ teaspoon black pepper
$\frac{1}{8}$ teaspoon salt
3 cups torn stemmed washed spinach leaves

Cook beef in large saucepan over medium heat until no longer pink, stirring to separate meat. Rinse beef under warm water; drain. Return beef to saucepan; add water, stewed tomatoes with juice, carrots, onion, barley, bouillon granules, thyme, oregano, garlic powder, pepper and salt.

Bring to a boil over high heat. Reduce heat to medium-low. Cover and simmer 12 to 15 minutes or until barley and vegetables are tender, stirring occasionally. Stir in spinach; cook until spinach starts to wilt.

Makes 4 servings

Tip: Fresh spinach leaves cook very quickly. Add them to this soup just before serving and cook them for only a minute until they lose their crispiness.

Ground Beef, Spinach and Barley Soup

Side Dishes

Savory Skillet Broccoli

1   **tablespoon BERTOLLI® Olive Oil**
6   **cups fresh broccoli florets or 1 pound green beans,**
     trimmed
1   **envelope LIPTON® RECIPE SECRETS® Golden Onion**
     Soup Mix *
1¹/₂ **cups water**

*Also terrific with LIPTON® RECIPE SECRETS® Onion Mushroom Soup Mix.

1. In 12-inch skillet, heat oil over medium-high heat and cook broccoli, stirring occasionally, 2 minutes.

2. Stir in soup mix blended with water. Bring to a boil over high heat.

3. Reduce heat to medium-low and simmer covered 6 minutes or until broccoli is tender.   *Makes 4 servings*

Prep Time: *5 minutes*
Cook Time: *10 minutes*

Savory Skillet Broccoli

Bacon and Maple Grits Puff

8 slices bacon
2 cups milk
1 1/4 cups water
1 cup quick-cooking grits
1/2 teaspoon salt
1/2 cup pure maple syrup
4 eggs
Fresh chives (optional)

1. Preheat oven to 350°F. Grease 1 1/2-quart round casserole or soufflé dish; set aside.

2. Cook bacon in large skillet over medium-high heat about 7 minutes or until crisp. Remove bacon to paper towel; set aside. Reserve 2 tablespoons bacon drippings.

3. Combine milk, water, grits and salt in medium saucepan. Bring to a boil over medium heat, stirring frequently. Simmer 2 to 3 minutes or until mixture thickens, stirring constantly. Remove from heat; stir in syrup and reserved 2 tablespoons bacon drippings.

4. Crumble bacon; reserve 1/4 cup for garnish. Stir remaining crumbled bacon into grits mixture.

5. Beat eggs in medium bowl. Gradually stir small amount of grits mixture into eggs, then stir back into remaining grits mixture. Pour into prepared casserole.

6. Bake 1 hour and 20 minutes or until knife inserted in center comes out clean. Top with reserved 1/4 cup bacon. Garnish with fresh chives, if desired. Serve immediately. *Makes 6 to 8 servings*

Note: Puff will fall slightly after removing from oven.

Bacon and Maple Grits Puff

Herbed Green Bean Casserole

1 cup freshly grated Parmesan cheese
$^3/_4$ cup dried bread crumbs, divided
2 teaspoons parsley flakes
2 teaspoons dried basil
1 teaspoon dried oregano
1 teaspoon garlic powder
$^1/_2$ teaspoon salt
$^1/_2$ teaspoon black pepper
$^1/_2$ teaspoon dried thyme
$^1/_2$ cup CRISCO® Oil
2 (14-ounce) cans green beans, drained

Preheat oven to 350°F.

Combine first 9 ingredients in a large bowl. Toss well. Add CRISCO® Oil to bread crumb mixture; stir well. Reserve 2 tablespoons bread crumb mixture for top of casserole. Combine green beans and bread crumb mixture in an ovenproof dish and sprinkle with the reserved crumb mixture.

Bake for about 30 minutes or until the top is golden and crispy.

Makes 8 servings

Tip: You can replace the canned beans with frozen or blanched and cooled fresh beans. The dried bread crumbs and herbs can be replaced with Italian-style bread crumbs.

Herbed Green Bean Casserole

Festive Cranberry Mold

$^1/_2$ cup water
1 package (6 ounces) raspberry-flavored gelatin
1 can (8 ounces) cranberry sauce
$1^2/_3$ cups cranberry juice cocktail
1 cup sliced bananas (optional)
$^1/_2$ cup walnuts, toasted (optional)

Bring water to a boil, in medium saucepan over medium-high heat. Add gelatin and stir until dissolved. Fold in cranberry sauce. Reduce heat to medium; cook until sauce is melted. Stir in cranberry juice cocktail.

Refrigerate mixture until slightly thickened. Fold in banana slices and walnuts, if desired. Pour mixture into 4-cup mold; cover and refrigerate until gelatin is set.

Makes 8 servings

Chunky Applesauce

10 tart apples (about 3 pounds) peeled, cored and chopped
$^3/_4$ cup packed light brown sugar
$^1/_2$ cup apple juice or apple cider
$1^1/_2$ teaspoons ground cinnamon
$^1/_8$ teaspoon salt
$^1/_8$ teaspoon ground nutmeg

1. Combine apples, brown sugar, apple juice, cinnamon, salt and nutmeg in heavy, large saucepan; cover. Cook over medium-low heat 40 to 45 minutes or until apples are tender, stirring occasionally. Remove saucepan from heat. Cool completely.

2. Store in airtight container in refrigerator up to 1 month.

Makes about $5^1/_2$ cups

Festive Cranberry Mold

Golden Corn Pudding

2 **tablespoons butter** or margarine
3 **tablespoons all-purpose flour**
1 **can (14³/₄ ounces) DEL MONTE® Cream Style Golden
    Sweet Corn**
¹/₄ **cup yellow cornmeal**
2 **eggs, separated**
1 **package (3 ounces) cream cheese, softened**
1 **can (8³/₄ ounces) DEL MONTE Whole Kernel Golden
    Sweet Corn, drained**

1. *Preheat oven to 350°F.*

2. *Melt butter in medium saucepan. Add flour and stir until smooth. Blend in cream style corn and cornmeal. Bring to a boil over medium heat, stirring constantly.*

3. *Place egg yolks in small bowl; stir in ¹/₂ cup hot mixture. Pour mixture back into saucepan. Add cream cheese and whole kernel corn.*

4. *Place egg whites in clean narrow bowl and beat until stiff peaks form. With rubber spatula, gently fold egg whites into corn mixture.*

5. *Pour mixture into 1¹/₂-quart straight-sided baking dish. Bake 30 to 35 minutes or until lightly browned.*   *Makes 4 to 6 servings*

Tip: *Pudding can be prepared up to 3 hours ahead of serving time. Cover and refrigerate until about 30 minutes before baking.*

Prep Time: *10 minutes*
Bake Time: *35 minutes*

Southern Hush Puppies

CRISCO® Oil,* for frying
3/4 cup yellow cornmeal
1/3 cup unsifted all-purpose flour
1 1/2 teaspoons baking powder
1/2 teaspoon salt
1/2 cup buttermilk
1 egg
1/4 cup finely chopped onion

*Use your favorite Crisco Oil product.

1. Heat 2 to 3 inches of oil in deep-fryer or large saucepan over high heat to 375°F.

2. Mix cornmeal, flour, baking powder and salt in medium mixing bowl. Add remaining ingredients; mix well.

3. Drop batter by tablespoonfuls into hot oil. Fry a few hush puppies at a time, 3 to 4 minutes, or until golden brown. Remove with slotted spoon.

4. Drain on paper towels. Repeat with remaining batter. Serve immediately or keep warm in 175°F oven.   *Makes about 1 dozen hush puppies*

Tip: Proper oil temperature is crucial to successful frying. The ideal temperature produces a crisp exterior and a moist, perfectly cooked interior.

Zucchini Delight

    1 can (10³/₄ ounces) condensed reduced-fat tomato
        soup, undiluted
    1 tablespoon lemon juice
    1 teaspoon sugar
    2 cloves garlic, minced
  ¹/₂ teaspoon salt
    6 cups ¹/₂-inch zucchini slices
    1 cup thinly sliced onion
    1 cup coarsely chopped green bell pepper
    1 cup sliced mushrooms
    2 tablespoons grated Parmesan cheese

Combine soup, lemon juice, sugar, garlic and salt in large saucepan; mix well. Add zucchini, onion, bell pepper and mushrooms; mix well. Bring to a boil; reduce heat. Cover and cook 20 to 25 minutes or until vegetables are crisp-tender, stirring occasionally. Sprinkle with cheese before serving.

Makes 6 servings

Apricot Carrots

    1 pound peeled mini carrots
    2 tablespoons water
  ¹/₂ cup SMUCKER'S® Apricot Preserves
    1 tablespoon butter or margarine, melted
    1 tablespoon lemon juice
  ¹/₂ teaspoon salt
  ¹/₈ teaspoon ground mace

1. Cook carrots, covered, in 2 tablespoons of boiling water for about 8 minutes or until tender. Drain thoroughly; return to pan.

2. Combine preserves, butter, lemon juice, salt and mace. Pour over cooked carrots. Cook, stirring constantly until carrots are evenly glazed and heated through.

Makes 4 servings

Zucchini Delight

Broccoli Casserole with Crumb Topping

    2 slices day-old white bread, coarsely crumbled
        (about 1¼ cups)
    ½ cup shredded mozzarella cheese (about 2 ounces)
    2 tablespoons chopped fresh parsley (optional)
    2 tablespoons BERTOLLI® Olive Oil
    1 clove garlic, finely chopped
    6 cups broccoli florets and/or cauliflowerets
    1 envelope LIPTON® RECIPE SECRETS® Onion Soup
        Mix
    1 cup water
    1 large tomato, chopped

1. In small bowl, combine bread crumbs, cheese, parsley, 1 tablespoon oil and garlic; set aside.

2. In 12-inch skillet, heat remaining 1 tablespoon oil over medium heat and cook broccoli, stirring frequently, 2 minutes.

3. Stir in onion soup mix blended with water. Bring to a boil over high heat. Reduce heat to low and simmer uncovered, stirring occasionally, 8 minutes or until broccoli is almost tender. Add tomato and simmer 2 minutes.

4. Spoon vegetable mixture into 1½-quart casserole; top with bread crumb mixture. Broil 1½ minutes or until crumbs are golden and cheese is melted.

Makes 6 servings

Broccoli Casserole with Crumb Topping

Swiss-Style Vegetables

$^3/_4$ **cup cubed unpeeled red potato**
2 **cups broccoli florets**
1 **cup cauliflower florets**
2 **teaspoons margarine**
1 **cup sliced mushrooms**
1 **tablespoon all-purpose flour**
1 **cup half-and-half**
$^1/_2$ **cup shredded Swiss cheese**
$^1/_4$ **teaspoon salt**
$^1/_4$ **teaspoon black pepper**
$^1/_4$ **teaspoon hot pepper sauce (optional)**
$^1/_8$ **teaspoon ground nutmeg**
$^1/_4$ **cup grated Parmesan cheese**

1. Place potato in medium saucepan; cover with cold water. Bring water to a boil. Reduce heat; cover and simmer 10 minutes. Add broccoli and cauliflower; cover and cook about 5 minutes or until all vegetables are tender. Drain; remove vegetables and set aside.

2. Melt margarine in same pan over medium-low heat. Add mushrooms. Cook and stir 2 minutes. Stir in flour; cook 1 minute. Slowly stir in half-and-half; cook and stir until mixture thickens. Remove from heat. Add Swiss cheese, stirring until melted. Stir in salt, pepper, hot pepper sauce, if desired, and nutmeg.

3. Preheat broiler. Spray small shallow casserole with nonstick cooking spray.

4. Arrange vegetables in single layer in prepared casserole. Spoon sauce mixture over vegetables; sprinkle with Parmesan cheese.

5. Place casserole under broiler until cheese melts and browns, about 1 minute.   *Makes 6 ($^1/_2$-cup) servings*

Swiss-Style Vegetables

Country Green Beans with Turkey-Ham

2 teaspoons olive oil
1/4 cup minced onion
1 clove garlic, minced
1 pound fresh green beans, rinsed and drained
1 cup chopped fresh tomatoes
6 slices (2 ounces) thinly sliced low-fat smoked turkey-ham
1 tablespoon chopped fresh marjoram
2 teaspoons chopped fresh basil
1/8 teaspoon black pepper
1/4 cup herbed croutons

1. Heat oil in medium saucepan over medium heat. Add onion and garlic; cook and stir about 3 minutes or until onion is tender. Reduce heat to low.

2. Add green beans, tomatoes, turkey-ham, marjoram, basil and pepper. Cook about 10 minutes, stirring occasionally, until liquid from tomatoes is absorbed.

3. Transfer mixture to serving dish. Top with croutons.

Makes 4 servings

Honeyed Beets

1/4 cup unsweetened apple juice
2 tablespoons cider vinegar
1 tablespoon honey
2 teaspoons cornstarch
2 cans (8 ounces each) sliced beets, drained
Salt (optional)
Black pepper (optional)

Combine apple juice, vinegar, honey and cornstarch in large nonstick saucepan. Cook, stirring occasionally, over medium heat until simmering. Stir in beets and season to taste with salt and pepper, if desired. Simmer 3 minutes.

Makes 4 servings

Country Green Beans with Turkey-Ham

Asparagus with Dijon Mayonnaise

1 pound DOLE® Fresh Asparagus, trimmed
²/₃ cup fat-free or reduced-fat mayonnaise
2 tablespoons finely chopped DOLE® Green Onions
1 tablespoon lemon juice
1 tablespoon Dijon-style mustard
¹/₄ teaspoon prepared horseradish
Parsley (optional)

• Cook asparagus in boiling water 3 to 5 minutes or until tender-crisp; drain. Rinse in cold water; drain.

• Stir together mayonnaise, green onions, lemon juice, mustard and horseradish in bowl until blended. Garnish with parsley, if desired. Serve asparagus with dip.   *Makes 6 servings*

Garlic Mayonnaise: Omit mustard; stir in 2 garlic cloves, finely chopped and 2 tablespoons finely chopped fresh parsley.

Herb Mayonnaise: Omit mustard; stir in 2 tablespoons nonfat milk and ¹/₂ teaspoon each dill weed, dried basil leaves and dried rosemary.

Prep Time: 10 minutes
Cook Time: 5 minutes

Kentucky Cornbread & Sausage Stuffing

 $^1/_2$ **pound BOB EVANS® Original Recipe Roll Sausage**
 3 **cups fresh bread cubes, dried or toasted**
 3 **cups crumbled prepared cornbread**
 1 **large apple, peeled and chopped**
 1 **small onion, chopped**
 1 **cup chicken or turkey broth**
 2 **tablespoons minced fresh parsley**
 1 **teaspoon salt**
 1 **teaspoon rubbed sage or poultry seasoning**
 $^1/_4$ **teaspoon black pepper**

Crumble sausage into small skillet. Cook over medium heat until browned, stirring occasionally. Place sausage and drippings in large bowl. Add remaining ingredients; toss lightly. Use to stuff chicken loosely just before roasting. Or, place stuffing in greased 13×9-inch baking dish. Add additional broth for moister stuffing, if desired. Bake in 350°F oven 30 minutes. Leftover stuffing should be removed from bird and stored separately in refrigerator. Reheat thoroughly before serving.

Makes enough stuffing for 5-pound chicken, 8 servings

Serving Suggestion: *Double this recipe to stuff a 12- to 15-pound turkey.*

Sweet Potato Apple Bake

 3 **cups mashed cooked sweet potatoes**
 2 **to 3 medium apples, peeled, sliced**
   Ground cinnamon
 $^1/_2$ **cup apple jelly**

Preheat oven to 350°F. Spray 9-inch glass pie plate with nonstick cooking spray. Fill dish evenly with mashed sweet potatoes. Arrange apple slices on top. Sprinkle apples with cinnamon. Melt apple jelly over low heat in small saucepan. Brush over apples. Bake 30 minutes or until apples are tender.

Makes 6 servings

Favorite recipe from **New York Apple Association, Inc.**

Quick Breads

Cranberry Cheesecake Muffins

1 package (3 ounces) cream cheese, softened
4 tablespoons sugar, divided
1 cup reduced-fat (2%) milk
1/3 cup vegetable oil
1 egg
1 package (about 15 ounces) cranberry quick
    bread mix

1. Preheat oven to 400°F. Grease 12 muffin pan cups.

2. Beat cream cheese and 2 tablespoons sugar in small bowl until well blended; set aside.

3. Beat milk, oil and egg in large bowl until blended. Stir in quick bread mix just until dry ingredients are moistened.

4. Fill prepared muffin cups ¼ full with batter. Drop 1 teaspoon cream cheese mixture into center of each cup. Spoon remaining batter over cream cheese mixture.

5. Sprinkle batter with remaining 2 tablespoons sugar. Bake 17 to 22 minutes or until golden brown. Cool 5 minutes. Remove from muffin cups to wire rack to cool.   *Makes 12 muffins*

Prep and Bake Time: *30 minutes*

Cranberry Cheesecake Muffins

Cheddar-Apple Bread

2 cups all-purpose flour
2 teaspoons baking powder
1 teaspoon baking soda
$^1/_4$ teaspoon salt
1 cup packed light brown sugar
$^1/_2$ cup butter, softened
2 eggs
1 teaspoon vanilla
1 cup sour cream
$^1/_4$ cup milk
$1^1/_2$ cups diced dried apples
1 cup (4 ounces) shredded Cheddar cheese

1. Preheat oven to 350°F. Spray 9×5-inch loaf pan with nonstick cooking spray; set aside.

2. Combine flour, baking powder, baking soda and salt in small bowl. Beat sugar and butter in large bowl with electric mixer at medium speed until light and fluffy. Beat in eggs and vanilla until blended. Add flour mixture to butter mixture alternately with sour cream and milk, beginning and ending with flour mixture. Beat well after each addition. Stir in apples and cheese until blended. Spoon into prepared pan.

3. Bake 50 to 55 minutes or until toothpick inserted into center comes out clean. Cool in pan on wire rack 15 minutes. Remove from pan and cool completely on wire rack.   *Makes 12 servings*

Tip: Brown sugar can become hard during storage making it difficult to measure. To soften it, place the brown sugar in a microwavable bowl and microwave at HIGH 30 to 60 seconds or until softened.

Cheddar-Apple Bread

Calico Bell Pepper Muffins

$^1/_4$ **cup each finely chopped red, yellow and green bell pepper**
  2 **tablespoons margarine**
  2 **cups all-purpose flour**
  4 **tablespoons sugar**
  1 **tablespoon baking powder**
$^3/_4$ **teaspoon salt**
$^1/_2$ **teaspoon dried basil leaves**
  1 **cup low-fat milk**
  1 **whole egg**
  2 **egg whites**

Preheat oven to 400°F. Paper-line 12 muffin cups or spray with cooking spray. In small skillet, cook peppers in margarine over medium-high heat until color is bright and peppers are tender-crisp, about 3 minutes. Set aside.

In large bowl, combine flour, sugar, baking powder, salt and basil. In small bowl, combine milk, whole egg and egg whites until blended. Add milk mixture and peppers with drippings to flour mixture and stir until just moistened. Spoon into prepared muffin cups. Bake 15 minutes or until golden and wooden pick inserted in centers comes out clean. Cool briefly and remove from pan.   *Makes 12 muffins*

Favorite recipe from **The Sugar Association, Inc.**

Calico Bell Pepper Muffins

Old-Fashioned Cake Doughnuts

3³/₄ **cups all-purpose flour**
1 **tablespoon baking powder**
1 **teaspoon ground cinnamon**
³/₄ **teaspoon salt**
¹/₂ **teaspoon ground nutmeg**
3 **eggs**
³/₄ **cup granulated sugar**
1 **cup applesauce**
2 **tablespoons butter, melted**
2 **cups sifted powdered sugar**
3 **tablespoons milk**
¹/₂ **teaspoon vanilla**
1 **quart vegetable oil**
Colored sprinkles (optional)

1. Combine flour, baking powder, cinnamon, salt and nutmeg in medium bowl. Beat eggs in large bowl with electric mixer at high speed until frothy. Gradually beat in granulated sugar at high speed 4 minutes until thick and lemon colored. Reduce speed to low; beat in applesauce and butter.

2. Beat in flour mixture until well blended. Divide dough into halves. Pat each half into 5-inch square; wrap in plastic wrap. Refrigerate 3 hours or until well chilled.

3. To prepare glaze, stir together powdered sugar, milk and vanilla in small bowl until smooth. Cover; set aside.

4. Roll out 1 dough half to ³/₈-inch thickness. Cut dough with floured 3-inch doughnut cutter; repeat with remaining dough. Reserve doughnut holes. Reroll scraps; cut dough again. Pour oil into large Dutch oven. Heat oil over medium heat until deep-fry thermometer registers 375°F. Adjust heat as necessary to maintain temperature.

5. Cook doughnuts and holes in batches 2 minutes or until golden brown, turning often. Remove with slotted spoon; drain on paper towels. Spread glaze over warm doughnuts; decorate with sprinkles, if desired.

Makes 12 doughnuts and holes

Old-Fashioned Cake Doughnuts

Country Buttermilk Biscuits

2 cups all-purpose flour
1 tablespoon baking powder
2 teaspoons sugar
$^1/_2$ teaspoon baking soda
$^1/_2$ teaspoon salt
$^1/_3$ cup shortening
$^2/_3$ cup buttermilk or sour milk*

To sour milk, place 2$^1/_2$ teaspoons lemon juice plus enough milk to equal $^2/_3$ cup in 1-cup measure. Stir; let stand 5 minutes before using.

1. Preheat oven to 450°F.

2. Combine flour, baking powder, sugar, baking soda and salt in medium bowl. Cut in shortening with pastry blender or 2 knives until mixture resembles coarse crumbs. Make well in center of dry ingredients. Add buttermilk; stir until mixture forms soft dough that clings together and forms ball.

3. Turn out dough onto well-floured surface. Knead dough gently 10 to 12 times. Roll or pat dough to $^1/_2$-inch thickness. Cut out dough with floured 2$^1/_2$-inch biscuit cutter.

4. Place biscuits 2 inches apart on ungreased large baking sheet. Bake 8 to 10 minutes or until tops and bottoms are golden brown. Serve warm.

Makes about 9 biscuits

Drop Biscuits: Prepare Country Buttermilk Biscuits as directed in steps 1 and 2, except increase buttermilk to 1 cup. After adding buttermilk, stir batter with wooden spoon about 15 strokes. Do not knead. Drop dough by heaping tablespoonfuls, 1 inch apart, onto greased baking sheets. Bake as directed in step 4. Makes about 18 biscuits.

Sour Cream Dill Biscuits: Prepare Country Buttermilk Biscuits as directed in steps 1 through 2, except omit buttermilk. Combine $^1/_2$ cup sour cream, $^1/_3$ cup milk and 1 tablespoon chopped fresh dill or 1 teaspoon dried dill weed, in small bowl until well blended. Stir into dry ingredients and continue as directed in steps 3 and 4. Makes about 9 biscuits.

continued on page 120

Country Buttermilk Biscuits

Country Buttermilk Biscuits, continued

Bacon 'n' Onion Biscuits: *Prepare Country Buttermilk Biscuits as directed in steps 1 through 2, except add 4 slices crumbled crisp-cooked bacon (about $^1/_3$ cup) and $^1/_3$ cup chopped green onions (about 3 onions) to flour-shortening mixture before adding buttermilk. Continue as directed in steps 3 and 4. Makes about 9 biscuits.*

Date Nut Bread

             2 **cups all-purpose flour**
     $^1/_2$ **cup packed light brown sugar**
             1 **tablespoon baking powder**
     $^1/_2$ **teaspoon salt**
     $^1/_4$ **cup cold butter**
             1 **cup toasted chopped walnuts**
             1 **cup chopped dates**
    $1^1/_4$ **cups milk**
             1 **egg**
     $^1/_2$ **teaspoon grated lemon peel**

1. Preheat oven to 375°F. Spray 9×5-inch loaf pan with nonstick cooking spray; set aside.

2. Combine flour, brown sugar, baking powder and salt in large bowl. Cut in butter with pastry blender or 2 knives until mixture resembles fine crumbs. Add walnuts and dates; stir until coated. Beat milk, egg and lemon peel in small bowl with fork. Add to flour mixture; stir just until moistened. Pour into prepared pan.

3. Bake 45 to 50 minutes or until toothpick inserted into center comes out clean. Cool in pan on wire rack 10 minutes. Remove from pan and cool completely on wire rack. *Makes 12 servings*

Tip: *Dates can be chopped with a chef's knife or cut into small pieces using kitchen shears. Lightly spray the knife or shears with nonstick cooking spray to prevent the dates from sticking.*

Blueberry Coffee Cake

Coffee Cake
$1\frac{1}{2}$ cups all-purpose flour, divided
$\frac{1}{4}$ cup granulated sugar
$2\frac{1}{2}$ teaspoons baking powder
$\frac{1}{2}$ teaspoon salt
$\frac{1}{4}$ teaspoon ground allspice
$\frac{2}{3}$ cup milk
$\frac{1}{3}$ cup butter or margarine, melted
1 egg
$\frac{3}{4}$ cup SMUCKER'S® Blueberry Preserves

Topping
$\frac{1}{4}$ cup firmly packed brown sugar
$\frac{1}{4}$ cup chopped walnuts
2 tablespoons all-purpose flour
1 tablespoon butter or margarine

Preheat oven to 400°F. Grease and flour 8- or 9-inch square baking pan. Lightly spoon flour into measuring cup; level off.

In medium bowl, combine 1 cup flour, granulated sugar, baking powder, salt and allspice. Add milk, melted butter and egg. Mix vigorously until well blended.

Pour half of batter into greased and floured pan; spread SMUCKER'S® preserves evenly over batter. Top with remaining batter.

Combine topping ingredients; mix until crumbly. Sprinkle over top of coffee cake batter.

Bake for 20 to 25 minutes or until toothpick inserted in center comes out clean.

Makes 9 servings

Ham and Cheese Corn Muffins

1 **package (about 8 ounces) corn muffin mix**
½ **cup chopped deli ham**
½ **cup (2 ounces) shredded Swiss cheese**
⅓ **cup reduced-fat (2%) milk**
1 **egg**
1 **tablespoon Dijon mustard**

1. *Preheat oven to 400°F. Line 9 (2¾-inch) muffin cups with paper cups.*

2. *Combine muffin mix, ham and cheese in medium bowl.*

3. *Beat milk, egg and mustard in 1-cup glass measure. Stir milk mixture into dry ingredients; mix just until moistened.*

4. *Fill muffin cups two-thirds full with batter. Bake 18 to 20 minutes or until light golden brown. Remove muffin pan to cooling rack. Let stand 5 minutes. Serve muffins warm.*　　　　　　　　*Makes 9 muffins*

Serving Suggestion: *For added flavor, serve Ham and Cheese Corn Muffins with honey-flavored butter. To prepare, stir together equal amounts of honey and softened butter.*

Prep and Cook Time: *30 minutes*

Tip: *When making muffin batter, stir it just until the dry ingredients are moistened. The batter will be lumpy, but the lumps will disappear during baking. Overmixing will result in muffins with a tough texture.*

Ham and Cheese Corn Muffins

Cherry Zucchini Bread

2 eggs
$^3/_4$ cup sugar
$^1/_3$ cup vegetable oil
$^1/_3$ cup lemon juice
$^1/_4$ cup water
2 cups all-purpose flour
2 teaspoons baking powder
1 teaspoon ground cinnamon
$^1/_2$ teaspoon baking soda
$^1/_4$ teaspoon salt
$^2/_3$ cup shredded unpeeled zucchini
$^2/_3$ cup dried tart cherries
1 tablespoon grated lemon peel

Put eggs in large mixing bowl. Beat with an electric mixer on medium speed 3 to 4 minutes or until eggs are thick and lemon colored. Add sugar, oil, lemon juice and water; mix well. Combine flour, baking powder, cinnamon, baking soda and salt. Add flour mixture to egg mixture; mix well. Stir in zucchini, cherries and lemon peel.

Grease and flour bottom of $8^1/_2 \times 4^1/_2$-inch loaf pan. Pour batter into prepared pan. Bake in preheated 350°F oven 55 to 65 minutes or until wooden toothpick inserted in center comes out clean. Let cool in pan on wire rack 10 minutes. Loosen edges with a metal spatula. Remove from pan. Let cool completely. Wrap tightly in plastic wrap and store in refrigerator.

Makes 1 loaf, about 16 servings

Favorite recipe from **Cherry Marketing Institute**

Cherry Zucchini Bread

Grandma's® Bran Muffins

2¹/₂ **cups bran flakes, divided**
1 **cup raisins**
1 **cup boiling water**
2 **cups buttermilk**
1 **cup GRANDMA'S® Molasses**
¹/₂ **cup canola oil**
2 **eggs, beaten**
2³/₄ **cups all-purpose flour**
2¹/₂ **teaspoons baking soda**
¹/₂ **teaspoon salt**

Heat oven to 400°F. In medium bowl, mix 1 cup bran flakes, raisins and water. Set aside. In large bowl, combine remaining ingredients. Stir in bran-raisin mixture. Pour into greased muffin pan cups. Fill ²/₃ full and bake for 20 minutes. Remove muffins and place on rack to cool.

Makes 48 muffins

Peach and Sausage Waffles

¹/₂ **pound BOB EVANS® Original Recipe Roll Sausage**
1 **cup all-purpose flour**
3 **tablespoons sugar**
2 **teaspoons baking powder**
2 **eggs**
2 **cups milk**
4 **tablespoons melted butter**
1 **cup chopped, drained canned peaches**

Preheat waffle iron. If preparing waffles in advance, preheat oven to 200°F. Crumble and cook sausage in medium skillet until browned; drain on paper towels. Whisk flour, sugar and baking powder in large bowl. Whisk eggs and milk in medium bowl until well blended. Pour liquid ingredients over dry ingredients; whisk until just combined. Stir in butter until blended. Stir in peaches and sausage. Lightly butter grids of waffle iron; add ¹/₂ cup batter to hot iron. Cook waffles according to manufacturer's instructions. Serve immediately or hold in oven until ready to serve.   *Makes 6 servings*

Grandma's® Bran Muffins

Buttermilk Corn Bread Loaf

1½ cups all-purpose flour
1 cup yellow cornmeal
⅓ cup sugar
2 teaspoons baking powder
1 teaspoon salt
½ teaspoon baking soda
½ cup shortening
1⅓ cups buttermilk*
2 eggs

*To sour milk, place 4 teaspoons lemon juice plus enough milk to equal 1⅓ cups in 2-cup measure. Stir; let stand 5 minutes before using.

1. Preheat oven to 375°F. Grease 8½×4½-inch loaf pan; set aside.

2. Combine flour, cornmeal, sugar, baking powder, salt and baking soda in medium bowl. Cut in shortening with pastry blender or 2 knives until mixture resembles coarse crumbs.

3. Whisk together buttermilk and eggs in small bowl. Make well in center of dry ingredients. Add buttermilk mixture; stir until mixture forms stiff batter. (Batter will be lumpy.) Turn into prepared pan; spread mixture evenly, removing any air bubbles.

4. Bake 50 to 55 minutes or until toothpick inserted in center comes out clean. Cool in pan on wire rack 10 minutes. Remove from pan; cool on rack 10 minutes more. Serve warm. *Makes 1 loaf (12 slices)*

Buttermilk Corn Bread Loaf

Pumpkin Streusel Coffeecake

Streusel Topping
- $^1/_2$ **cup all-purpose flour**
- $^1/_4$ **cup packed brown sugar**
- 1$^1/_2$ **teaspoons ground cinnamon**
- 3 **tablespoons butter or margarine**
- $^1/_2$ **cup coarsely chopped nuts**

Coffeecake
- 2 **cups all-purpose flour**
- 2 **teaspoons baking powder**
- 1$^1/_2$ **teaspoons ground cinnamon**
- $^1/_2$ **teaspoon baking soda**
- $^1/_4$ **teaspoon salt**
- 1 **cup (2 sticks) butter or margarine, softened**
- 1 **cup granulated sugar**
- 2 **eggs**
- 1 **cup LIBBY'S® 100% Pure Pumpkin**
- 1 **teaspoon vanilla extract**

PREHEAT *oven to 350°F. Grease and flour 9-inch-round cake pan.*

For Streusel Topping
COMBINE *flour, brown sugar and cinnamon in medium bowl. Cut in butter with pastry blender or two knives until mixture is crumbly; stir in nuts.*

For Coffeecake
COMBINE *flour, baking powder, cinnamon, baking soda and salt in small bowl. Beat butter and granulated sugar in large mixer bowl until creamy. Add eggs, one at a time, beating well after each addition. Beat in pumpkin and vanilla extract. Gradually beat in flour mixture.*

SPOON *half of batter into prepared cake pan. Sprinkle half of Streusel Topping over batter. Spoon remaining batter evenly over Streusel Topping; sprinkle with remaining Streusel Topping.*

BAKE *for 45 to 50 minutes or until wooden pick inserted in center comes out clean. Cool in pan on wire rack for 10 minutes; remove to wire rack to cool completely.*   *Makes 10 servings*

Honey Soda Bread

2 cups all-purpose flour
1 cup whole wheat flour
2 teaspoons baking soda
1/2 teaspoon salt
1/4 cup butter or margarine, cut up
1 cup golden raisins
2 teaspoons caraway seeds
1 cup plain low-fat yogurt
1/3 cup honey
2 tablespoons milk

In large bowl, combine flours, baking soda and salt; mix well. Cut in butter until mixture resembles coarse crumbs; mix in raisins and caraway seeds.

In small bowl, whisk together yogurt and honey. Add to flour mixture; stir until just combined. Turn dough onto lightly floured surface; knead 10 times or until dough is smooth. Form dough into ball; place on lightly greased baking sheet. With sharp knife, cut an "X" 1/4 inch deep into top of loaf; brush with milk. Bake at 325°F for 45 to 50 minutes, or until golden. Cool on wire rack.

Makes 1 loaf

Favorite recipe from **National Honey Board**

Tip: Whole wheat flour is more perishable than other types of flour, so purchase it in small amounts and store it in the refrigerator for no more than 3 months. Allow chilled flour to return to room temperature before using it.

Cakes and Pies

Lemon Dream Pie

- 1 prepared or homemade 9-inch pie shell
- 1 1/2 cups water
- 1 cup honey
- 1/2 cup lemon juice
- 1/3 cup cornstarch
- 2 tablespoons butter or margarine
- 1 teaspoon grated lemon peel
- 1/4 teaspoon salt
- 4 egg yolks, lightly beaten
- 1 1/2 cups heavy whipping cream, whipped to soft peaks

Bake empty pie shell according to package directions until golden brown. In medium saucepan, combine water, honey, lemon juice, cornstarch, butter, lemon peel and salt. Bring to a boil, stirring constantly. Boil for 5 minutes. Remove from heat. Stir small amount of honey mixture into yolks. Pour yolk mixture back into honey mixture; mix thoroughly. Pour into pie shell. Chill. To serve, top with whipped cream. *Makes 8 servings*

Favorite recipe from **National Honey Board**

Lemon Dream Pie

Chocolate Fudge Pie

Crust
  1 unbaked Classic Crisco® Single Crust (page 139)

Filling
  $^1/_4$ **CRISCO® Stick or $^1/_4$ cup CRISCO® all-vegetable
      shortening**
  1 **bar (4 ounces) sweet baking chocolate**
  1 **can (14 ounces) sweetened condensed milk**
  $^1/_2$ **cup all-purpose flour**
  2 **eggs, beaten**
  1 **teaspoon vanilla**
  $^1/_4$ **teaspoon salt**
  1 **cup flake coconut**
  1 **cup chopped pecans**

Garnish
  Unsweetened whipped cream or ice cream

1. *For crust, prepare as directed. Do not bake. Heat oven to 350°F. Place wire rack on countertop for cooling pie.*

2. *For filling, melt $^1/_4$ cup shortening and chocolate in heavy saucepan over low heat. Remove from heat. Stir in sweetened condensed milk, flour, eggs, vanilla and salt; mix well. Stir in coconut and nuts. Pour into unbaked pie crust.*

3. *Bake at 350°F for 40 minutes or until toothpick inserted into center comes out clean. Cool completely on wire rack.*

4. *Serve with unsweetened whipped cream or ice cream, if desired. Refrigerate leftover pie.*   *Makes 1 (9-inch) pie (8 servings)*

Prep Time: *about 30 minutes*
Bake Time: *about 40 minutes*

Chocolate Fudge Pie

Orange Glazed Pound Cake

1 package DUNCAN HINES® Moist Deluxe® Butter
   Recipe Golden Cake Mix
4 eggs
1 cup sour cream
1/3 cup vegetable oil
1/4 cup plus 1 to 2 tablespoons orange juice, divided
2 tablespoons grated orange peel
1 cup confectioners' sugar

1. Preheat oven to 375°F. Grease and flour 10-inch tube pan.

2. Combine cake mix, eggs, sour cream, oil, 1/4 cup orange juice and orange peel in large bowl. Beat at medium speed with electric mixer for 2 minutes. Pour into prepared pan. Bake at 375°F for 45 to 50 minutes or until toothpick inserted in center comes out clean. Cool in pan 25 minutes. Invert onto cooling rack. Cool completely.

3. Combine sugar and remaining 1 to 2 tablespoons orange juice in small bowl; stir until smooth. Drizzle over cake. Garnish as desired.

Makes 12 to 16 servings

Coconut Cream Pie

1 package (4-serving size) instant vanilla-flavored
   pudding mix
2 3/4 cups cold milk, divided
1 prepared (9-inch) graham cracker pie crust
1 envelope whipped topping mix
1/2 teaspoon vanilla
1 package (4 ounces) flaked coconut

1. Beat pudding mix and 1 3/4 cups milk in medium bowl with electric mixer until thick. Pour into pie crust and refrigerate 1 hour.

2. Beat remaining 1 cup milk, whipped topping mix and vanilla with electric mixer in large bowl. Beat 4 minutes at high or until thick and fluffy, spread on pie. Sprinkle coconut evenly on pie. Refrigerate until ready to serve.

Makes 8 servings

Orange Glazed Pound Cake

Golden Ambrosia Pecan Pie

Crust
>   *Classic CRISCO® Single Crust (page 139)*

Filling
> 3 **eggs, beaten**
> ³/₄ **cup light corn syrup**
> ¹/₂ **cup granulated sugar**
> 3 **tablespoons firmly packed light brown sugar**
> 2 **tablespoons butter or margarine, melted**
> 3 **tablespoons thawed frozen orange juice**
>   **concentrate**
> 2 **tablespoons cornstarch**
> 1 **teaspoon grated orange peel**
> 1 **teaspoon vanilla**
> ¹/₂ **teaspoon coconut extract or flavor**
> 1¹/₂ **cups chopped pecans**
> ²/₃ **cup flaked coconut**

1. For crust, prepare as directed. Do not bake. Heat oven to 350°F.

2. For filling, combine eggs, corn syrup, sugars and butter in large bowl. Stir well. Combine orange juice concentrate, cornstarch, orange peel, vanilla and coconut extract. Add to egg mixture. Stir well. Stir in nuts and coconut. Pour into unbaked pie crust. Cover edge with foil to prevent overbrowning.

3. Bake at 350°F for 35 minutes. Remove foil. Bake for 15 to 20 minutes or until set and crust is golden brown. Do not overbake. Cool to room temperature before serving. Garnish as desired.

Makes 1 (9-inch) pie (8 servings)

Classic Crisco® Single Crust

1¹/₃ **cups all-purpose flour**
¹/₂ **teaspoon salt**
¹/₂ **CRISCO® Stick or** ¹/₂ **cup CRISCO® all-vegetable
    shortening**
 3 **tablespoons cold water**

1. Spoon flour into measuring cup and level. Combine flour and salt in medium bowl.

2. Cut in ¹/₂ cup shortening using pastry blender or 2 knives until all flour is blended to form pea-size chunks.

3. Sprinkle with water, 1 tablespoon at a time. Toss lightly with fork until dough forms a ball.

4. Press dough between hands to form 5- to 6-inch "pancake." Flour rolling surface and rolling pin lightly. Roll dough into circle. Trim circle 1 inch larger than upside-down pie plate. Carefully remove trimmed dough.

5. Fold dough into quarters. Unfold and press into pie plate. Fold edge under; flute edges.

6. **For recipes using a baked pie crust,** heat oven to 425°F. Prick bottom and side thoroughly with fork (50 times) to prevent shrinkage. Bake at 425°F for 10 to 15 minutes or until lightly browned.

7. **For recipes using an unbaked pie crust,** follow directions given for that recipe.   *Makes 1 (9-inch) single crust*

Hershey's Red Velvet Cake

$^1/_2$ cup (1 stick) butter or margarine, softened
$1^1/_2$ cups sugar
2 eggs
1 teaspoon vanilla extract
1 cup buttermilk or sour milk*
2 tablespoons (1-ounce bottle) red food color
2 cups all-purpose flour
$^1/_3$ cup HERSHEY'S Cocoa
1 teaspoon salt
$1^1/_2$ teaspoons baking soda
1 tablespoon white vinegar
1 can (16 ounces) ready-to-spread vanilla frosting
HERSHEY'S MINI CHIPS™ Semi-Sweet Chocolate
Chips or HERSHEY'S Milk Chocolate Chips
(optional)

*To sour milk: Use 1 tablespoon white vinegar plus milk to equal 1 cup.

1. Heat oven to 350°F. Grease and flour 13×9×2-inch baking pan.**

2. Beat butter and sugar in large bowl; add eggs and vanilla, beating well. Stir together buttermilk and food color. Stir together flour, cocoa and salt; add alternately to butter mixture with buttermilk mixture, mixing well. Stir in baking soda and vinegar. Pour into prepared pan.

3. Bake 30 to 35 minutes or until wooden pick inserted in center comes out clean. Cool completely in pan on wire rack. Frost; garnish with chocolate chips, if desired.   Makes about 15 servings

**This recipe can be made in 2 (9-inch) cake pans. Bake at 350°F for 30 to 35 minutes.

Hershey's Red Velvet Cake

Deep-Dish Peach Custard Pie

     1 unbaked 9-inch (4-cup volume) deep-dish pie shell
  3¹/₂ cups (about 7 medium) peeled, pitted and sliced
        peaches
     1 can (14 ounces) NESTLÉ® CARNATION® Sweetened
        Condensed Milk
     2 large eggs
   ¹/₄ cup butter or margarine, melted
     1 to 3 teaspoons lemon juice
   ¹/₂ teaspoon ground cinnamon
        Dash ground nutmeg
        Streusel Topping (recipe follows)

PREHEAT *oven to 425°F.*

ARRANGE *peaches in pie shell. Combine sweetened condensed milk, eggs, butter, lemon juice, cinnamon and nutmeg in large mixer bowl; beat until smooth. Pour over peaches.*

BAKE *for 10 minutes. Sprinkle with Streusel Topping. Reduce oven temperature to 350°F; bake for additional 55 to 60 minutes or until knife inserted near center comes out clean. Cool on wire rack.*

Makes 8 servings

Streusel Topping: **COMBINE** *¹/₃ cup packed brown sugar, ¹/₃ cup all-purpose flour and ¹/₃ cup chopped walnuts in medium bowl. Cut in 2 tablespoons butter or margarine with pastry blender or two knives until mixture resembles coarse crumbs.*

Deep-Dish Peach Custard Pie

Toffee-Topped Pineapple Upside-Down Cakes

$^1/_4$ **cup light corn syrup**
$^1/_4$ **cup ($^1/_2$ stick) butter or margarine, melted**
1 **cup HEATH® BITS 'O BRICKLE® or SKOR® English Toffee Bits**
4 **pineapple rings**
4 **maraschino cherries**
$^1/_4$ **cup ($^1/_2$ stick) butter or margarine, softened**
$^2/_3$ **cup sugar**
1 **egg**
1 **tablespoon rum or 1 teaspoon rum extract**
$1^1/_3$ **cups all-purpose flour**
2 **teaspoons baking powder**
$^2/_3$ **cup milk**

1. Heat oven to 350°F. Lightly coat inside of 4 individual 2-cup baking dishes with vegetable oil spray.

2. Stir together 1 tablespoon corn syrup and 4 tablespoons melted butter in each of 4 baking dishes. Sprinkle each with $^1/_4$ cup toffee. Center pineapple rings on toffee and place cherries in centers.

3. Beat softened butter and sugar in small bowl until blended. Add egg and rum, beating well. Stir together flour and baking powder; add alternately with milk to butter-sugar mixture, beating until smooth. Spoon about $^3/_4$ cup batter into each prepared dish.

4. Bake 25 to 30 minutes or until wooden pick inserted in centers comes out clean. Immediately invert onto serving dish. Refrigerate leftovers.

Makes four 4-inch cakes

Texas Chocolate Peanut Butter Pie

Crust
1 1/2 cups graham cracker crumbs
1/2 cup sugar
1/2 cup (1 stick) butter, melted

Filling
16 ounces cream cheese, at room temperature
2 cups creamy peanut butter
1 3/4 cups sugar
1 cup heavy whipping cream

Topping
2/3 cup heavy whipping cream
1/3 cup sugar
3 ounces semisweet chocolate
1/2 cup (1 stick) butter
1 teaspoon vanilla extract

For crust, preheat oven to 350°F. Combine graham cracker crumbs with sugar and melted butter. Stir until thoroughly blended. Press mixture into bottom and up side of 10-inch pie plate. Bake crust for 10 minutes; set aside to cool.

For filling, mix cream cheese, peanut butter and sugar in medium bowl until blended. Whip cream until stiff, then fold into cream cheese mixture. Spoon filling into cooled crust.

For topping, combine cream and sugar in saucepan and bring to a boil. Reduce heat and simmer for 7 minutes. Remove pan from heat. Add chocolate and butter; stir until melted. Stir in vanilla. Cool until slightly thickened. Pour evenly over pie. Refrigerate 4 to 5 hours before serving. Garnish with toasted peanuts.   *Makes one 10-inch pie (8 to 10 servings)*

Favorite recipe from **Texas Peanut Producers Board**

All-American Apple Pie

1 unbaked Classic CRISCO® Double Crust
   (page 148)
6 medium cooking apples
¾ cup granulated sugar
2 tablespoons all-purpose flour
1 teaspoon ground cinnamon
1 tablespoon butter or margarine
1 egg white, lightly beaten

Garnish
1 unbaked Classic CRISCO® Single Crust
   (page 139)

Preheat oven to 400°F.

Prepare pie crust; set aside.

For filling, peel, core and slice apples; toss with mixture of sugar, flour and cinnamon. Pour into unbaked pie crust; dot with butter.

Cover with top crust; seal and flute edge. Brush with egg white. Cut slits for steam to escape.

Roll additional crust to ⅛-inch thickness. With small 1½-inch star cookie cutter, cut 20 to 25 stars. Place 1 star on rim of top crust; brush with egg white. Repeat until rim is covered.

Bake for 30 to 40 minutes, until pie is golden brown and apples are tender.

Makes 1 (9-inch) pie

All-American Apple Pie

Classic Crisco® Double Crust

2 cups all-purpose flour
1 teaspoon salt
3/4 CRISCO® Stick or 3/4 cup CRISCO® all-vegetable
    shortening
5 tablespoons cold water (or more as needed)

1. Spoon flour into measuring cup and level. Combine flour and salt in medium bowl.

2. Cut in 3/4 cup shortening using pastry blender or 2 knives until all flour is blended to form pea-size chunks.

3. Sprinkle with water, 1 tablespoon at a time. Toss lightly with fork until dough forms a ball. Divide dough in half.

4. Press dough between hands to form two 5- to 6-inch "pancakes." Flour rolling surface and rolling pin lightly. Roll both halves of dough into circle. Trim one circle of dough 1 inch larger than upside-down pie plate. Carefully remove trimmed dough. Set aside to reroll and use for pastry cutout garnish, if desired.

5. Fold dough into quarters. Unfold and press into pie plate. Trim edge even with plate. Add desired filling to unbaked crust. Moisten pastry edge with water. Lift top crust onto filled pie. Trim 1/2 inch beyond edge of pie plate. Fold top edge under bottom crust. Flute. Cut slits in top crust to allow steam to escape. Follow baking directions given for that recipe.

Makes 1 (9-inch) double crust

Chocolate Sheet Cake

1¼ cups (2½ sticks) butter or margarine, divided
1 cup water
½ cup unsweetened cocoa, divided
2 cups all-purpose flour
1½ cups firmly packed light brown sugar
1 teaspoon baking soda
1 teaspoon ground cinnamon
½ teaspoon salt
1 (14-ounce) can EAGLE BRAND® Sweetened
    Condensed Milk (NOT evaporated milk), divided
2 eggs
1 teaspoon vanilla extract
1 cup powdered sugar
1 cup coarsely chopped nuts

1. Preheat oven to 350°F. In small saucepan over medium heat, melt 1 cup butter; stir in water and ¼ cup cocoa. Bring to a boil; remove from heat. In large mixing bowl, combine flour, brown sugar, baking soda, cinnamon and salt. Add cocoa mixture; beat well. Stir in ⅓ cup Eagle Brand, eggs and vanilla. Pour into greased 15×10×1-inch jelly-roll pan. Bake 15 minutes or until cake springs back when lightly touched.

2. In small saucepan over medium heat, melt remaining ¼ cup butter; add remaining ¼ cup cocoa and remaining Eagle Brand. Stir in powdered sugar and nuts. Spread over warm cake.   Makes one 15×10-inch cake

Pumpkin Carrot Cake

2 cups all-purpose flour
2 teaspoons baking soda
2 teaspoons ground cinnamon
$^1/_2$ teaspoon salt
$^3/_4$ cup milk
$1^1/_2$ teaspoons lemon juice
3 eggs
$1^1/_4$ cups LIBBY'S® 100% Pure Pumpkin
$1^1/_2$ cups granulated sugar
$^1/_2$ cup packed brown sugar
$^1/_2$ cup vegetable oil
1 can (8 ounces) crushed pineapple, drained
1 cup (about 3 medium) grated carrots
1 cup flaked coconut
$1^1/_4$ cups chopped nuts, divided
Cream Cheese Frosting (recipe follows)

PREHEAT oven to 350°F. Grease two 9-inch-round baking pans.

COMBINE flour, baking soda, cinnamon and salt in small bowl. Combine milk and lemon juice in liquid measuring cup (mixture will appear curdled).

BEAT eggs, pumpkin, granulated sugar, brown sugar, oil, pineapple, carrots and milk mixture in large mixer bowl; mix well. Gradually add flour mixture; beat until combined. Stir in coconut and 1 cup nuts. Pour into prepared baking pans.

BAKE for 30 to 35 minutes or until wooden pick inserted in center comes out clean. Cool in pans for 15 minutes. Remove to wire racks to cool completely.

FROST between layers, on side and top of cake with Cream Cheese Frosting. Garnish with remaining nuts. Store in refrigerator.

Makes 12 servings

Cream Cheese Frosting: **COMBINE** 11 ounces softened cream cheese, $^1/_3$ cup softened butter and $3^1/_2$ cups sifted powdered sugar in large mixer bowl until fluffy. Add 1 teaspoon vanilla extract, 2 teaspoons orange juice and 1 teaspoon grated orange peel; beat until combined.

Pumpkin Carrot Cake

Zesty Lemon Pound Cake

1 cup (6 ounces) NESTLÉ® TOLL HOUSE® Premier
    White Morsels or 3 bars (6-ounce box)
    NESTLÉ® TOLL HOUSE® Premier White Baking
    Bars, broken into pieces
2¹/₂ cups all-purpose flour
1 teaspoon baking powder
¹/₂ teaspoon salt
1 cup (2 sticks) butter, softened
1¹/₂ cups granulated sugar
2 teaspoons vanilla extract
3 eggs
3 to 4 tablespoons grated lemon peel
    (about 3 medium lemons)
1¹/₃ cups buttermilk
1 cup powdered sugar
3 tablespoons fresh lemon juice

PREHEAT oven to 350°F. Grease and flour 12-cup bundt pan.

MELT morsels in medium, uncovered, microwave-safe bowl on MEDIUM-HIGH (70%) power for 1 minute. STIR. Morsels may retain some of their original shape. If necessary, microwave at additional 10- to 15-second intervals, stirring just until morsels are melted. Cool slightly.

COMBINE flour, baking powder and salt in small bowl. Beat butter, granulated sugar and vanilla extract in large mixer bowl until creamy. Beat in eggs, one at a time, beating well after each addition. Beat in lemon peel and melted morsels. Gradually beat in flour mixture alternately with buttermilk. Pour into prepared bundt pan.

BAKE for 50 to 55 minutes or until wooden pick inserted in cake comes out clean. Cool in pan on wire rack for 10 minutes. Combine powdered sugar and lemon juice in small bowl. Make holes in cake with wooden pick; pour half of lemon glaze over cake. Let stand for 5 minutes. Invert onto plate. Make holes in top of cake; pour remaining glaze over cake. Cool completely before serving.   *Makes 16 servings*

Zesty Lemon Pound Cake

Peanut Butter Delight Cake

Cake
1 cup granulated sugar
$^3/_4$ cup Butter Flavor CRISCO® Stick or $^3/_4$ cup Butter
    Flavor CRISCO® All-Vegetable Shortening, plus
    additional for greasing pan
$^3/_4$ cup JIF® Creamy Peanut Butter
$^1/_2$ cup firmly packed light brown sugar
$1^1/_2$ teaspoons vanilla
3 eggs
$2^3/_4$ cups all-purpose flour
2 teaspoons baking powder
1 teaspoon baking soda
$^1/_2$ teaspoon salt
1 cup buttermilk or sour milk*
$^3/_4$ cup chocolate syrup

Glaze
1 cup confectioners' sugar
$^1/_4$ cup chocolate syrup
1 teaspoon vanilla
    Water
2 to 4 tablespoons chopped dry-roasted peanuts

*To sour milk: Combine 1 tablespoon white vinegar plus enough milk to equal 1 cup. Stir. Set aside 5 minutes before using.

Preheat oven to 350°F. Grease 10-inch (12-cup) bundt pan with shortening and flour lightly.

For cake, combine granulated sugar, $^3/_4$ cup shortening, JIF® peanut butter and brown sugar in large bowl. Beat at low speed of electric mixer until creamy. Add vanilla and eggs, 1 at a time, beating well after each addition.

Combine flour, baking powder, baking soda and salt in medium bowl. Add to peanut butter mixture alternately with buttermilk, beating after each addition until well blended.

Spoon 2 cups batter into medium bowl. Stir in $^3/_4$ cup chocolate syrup. Spoon plain batter into pan. Spoon chocolate batter over plain batter. Do not mix.

continued on page 156

Peanut Butter Delight Cake

Peanut Butter Delight Cake, continued

Bake for 1 hour 10 minutes to 1 hour 20 minutes or until toothpick inserted near center comes out clean. (Cake will rise, then fall during baking.) Do not overbake. Cool 45 minutes on wire rack before removing from pan. Place cake, fluted side up, on serving plate. Cool completely.

For glaze, combine confectioners' sugar, $1/4$ cup chocolate syrup and vanilla in small bowl. Stir to blend. Add water, 1 drop at a time, until glaze is of desired consistency. Spoon over top of cake. Sprinkle with nuts.

Makes 12 to 16 servings

Honey Strawberry Tart

$1/3$ **cup honey**
1 **tablespoon lemon juice**
1 **baked or ready-to-eat 9-inch pie shell**
4 **cups halved fresh strawberries**
Mint sprigs for garnish (optional)

Combine honey and lemon juice in small bowl; mix well. Brush bottom of pie shell with mixture. Fill shell with strawberries. Drizzle remaining honey mixture over berries. Garnish with mint sprigs, if desired.

Makes 8 servings

Tip: Prepare honey glaze and strawberries. Fill shell and glaze strawberries just before serving to prevent shell from becoming soggy.

Favorite recipe from **National Honey Board**

Honey Strawberry Tart

Apple-Scotch Snack Cake

Topping
   ⅔ *cup quick or old fashioned oats*
   6 *tablespoons all-purpose flour*
   4 *tablespoons butter, softened*
   3 *tablespoons firmly packed brown sugar*

Cake
 2¼ *cups all-purpose flour*
   1 *cup quick or old fashioned oats*
   1 *tablespoon baking powder*
   ½ *teaspoon salt*
   1 *cup firmly packed brown sugar*
   2 *eggs*
 1¼ *cups milk*
   6 *tablespoons butter, melted and cooled*
   1 *teaspoon vanilla extract*
 1⅓ *cups peeled and finely chopped apple (about*
      2 small tart apples)
 1⅓ *cups NESTLÉ® TOLL HOUSE® Butterscotch Flavored*
      Morsels, divided
 1½ *teaspoons milk*
      Vanilla ice cream (optional)

PREHEAT *oven to 350°F. Grease bottom of 13×9-inch baking pan.*

For Topping

COMBINE *oats, flour, butter and brown sugar in small bowl. With clean fingers, mix until crumbly; set aside.*

For Cake

COMBINE *flour, oats, baking powder and salt in large bowl. Combine brown sugar and eggs with wire whisk. Whisk in 1¼ cups milk, melted butter and vanilla extract. Add to flour mixture all at once; add apples. Stir gently until just combined. Pour into pan. Sprinkle with 1 cup morsels; crumble topping evenly over morsels.*

BAKE *for 40 minutes or until golden brown and wooden pick inserted in center comes out with a few moist crumbs clinging to it. Remove from oven to wire rack. Microwave remaining ⅓ cup morsels and 1½ teaspoons milk* in small microwave-safe bowl. Microwave on HIGH (100%) power for 20 seconds; stir until smooth. Carefully drizzle over hot cake in pan. Cool in pan at least 30 minutes. Cut into squares; serve warm or at room temperature with ice cream. Store tightly covered at room temperature.

Makes 16 servings

Sour Cream Cherry Cake

    1 (9-ounce) package yellow cake mix
    1 egg
 1½ cups reduced-fat (2%) milk, divided
    1 (3½-ounce) package vanilla pudding mix
  ½ cup dairy sour cream
  ½ teaspoon grated lemon peel
    2 cups pitted Northwest fresh sweet cherries
    2 tablespoons currant jelly, melted
      Mint sprigs
    1 cup sweetened whipped cream (optional)

Prepare yellow cake according to package directions using egg and ½ cup milk. Pour batter into flan pan and bake according to package directions. Prepare vanilla pudding according to package directions using 1 cup milk; remove from heat and stir in sour cream and lemon peel. When cake is cool, fill with vanilla pudding. Top with cherries; brush with melted jelly. Garnish with mint. Serve with whipped cream, if desired.

Makes 8 servings

Favorite recipe from **Northwest Cherry Growers**

Key Lime Pie

3 eggs, separated
1 (14-ounce) can EAGLE BRAND® Sweetened
    Condensed Milk (NOT evaporated milk)
$^1/_2$ cup lime juice from concentrate
2 to 3 drops green food coloring (optional)
1 (9-inch) unbaked pastry shell
$^1/_2$ teaspoon cream of tartar
$^1/_3$ cup sugar

1. Preheat oven to 325°F. In medium mixing bowl, beat egg yolks; gradually beat in Eagle Brand and lime juice. Stir in food coloring, if desired. Pour into pastry shell.

2. Bake 30 minutes. Remove from oven. Increase oven temperature to 350°F.

3. Meanwhile, for meringue, with clean mixer, beat egg whites and cream of tartar to soft peaks. Gradually beat in sugar, 1 tablespoon at a time. Beat 4 minutes or until stiff, glossy peaks form and sugar is dissolved.

4. Immediately spread meringue over hot pie, carefully sealing to edge of crust to prevent meringue from shrinking. Bake 15 minutes. Cool 1 hour. Chill at least 3 hours. Store covered in refrigerator.   *Makes 8 servings*

Prep Time: 25 minutes
Bake Time: 45 minutes
Cool Time: 1 hour
Chill Time: 3 hours

Tip: Beaten egg whites will reach their fullest volume if they are at room temperature. They must also be free of egg yolks and water because fat and water will result in reduced volume.

Key Lime Pie

Pennsylvania Shoo-Fly Pie

Crust
Classic CRISCO® Single Crust (page 139)

Crumb Mixture
2 cups all-purpose flour
1/2 cup firmly packed light brown sugar
1/3 cup butter or margarine, softened

Liquid Mixture
1 cup boiling water
1 teaspoon baking soda
3/4 cup plus 2 tablespoons dark molasses
2 tablespoons light molasses

1. For crust, prepare as directed. Do not bake. Heat oven to 375°F.

2. For crumb mixture, combine flour, brown sugar and butter in bowl. Mix until fine crumbs form. Reserve 1/2 cup for topping.

3. For liquid mixture, combine water and baking soda in large bowl. Stir until foamy. Add dark and light molasses. Stir well until foamy. Pour into unbaked pie crust. Add crumb mixture. Stir slightly until mixed. Sprinkle reserved 1/2 cup crumbs on top. Bake at 375°F for 45 to 55 minutes or until set. Do not overbake. Cool until warm or room temperature before serving.

Makes 1 (9-inch) pie (8 servings)

German Chocolate Cake

1 (18¼-ounce) package chocolate cake mix
1 cup water
3 eggs
½ cup vegetable oil
1 (14-ounce) can EAGLE BRAND® Sweetened
   Condensed Milk (NOT evaporated milk), divided
3 tablespoons butter or margarine
1 egg yolk
⅓ cup chopped pecans
⅓ cup flaked coconut
1 teaspoon vanilla extract

1. Preheat oven to 350°F. Grease and flour 13×9-inch baking pan. In large mixing bowl, combine cake mix, water, 3 eggs, oil and ⅓ cup Eagle Brand. Beat at low speed of electric mixer until moistened; beat at high speed 2 minutes.

2. Pour into prepared pan. Bake 40 to 45 minutes or until wooden pick inserted near center comes out clean.

3. In small saucepan over medium heat, combine remaining Eagle Brand, butter and egg yolk. Cook and stir until thickened, about 6 minutes. Add pecans, coconut and vanilla; spread over warm cake. Store covered in refrigerator. *Makes 10 to 12 servings*

Prep Time: *15 minutes*
Bake Time: *40 to 45 minutes*

Desserts

Chilled Cherry Cheesecake

   4 chocolate graham crackers, crushed (1 cup crumbs)
  12 ounces Neufchatel cheese
   8 ounces vanilla sugar-free nonfat yogurt
  $^1/_4$ cup sugar
   1 teaspoon vanilla
   1 envelope unflavored gelatin
  $^1/_4$ cup cold water
   1 can (20 ounces) light cherry pie filling

1. Sprinkle cracker crumbs on bottom of 8-inch square baking pan. Beat cheese, yogurt, sugar and vanilla in medium bowl with electric mixer until smooth and creamy.

2. Sprinkle gelatin into water in small cup; let stand 2 minutes. Microwave at HIGH 40 seconds, stir and let stand 2 minutes or until gelatin is completely dissolved.

3. Gradually beat gelatin mixture into cheese mixture with electric mixer until well blended. Pour into prepared pan; refrigerate until firm. Spoon cherry topping onto cheesecake. Refrigerate until ready to serve.

Makes 9 servings

Chilled Cherry Cheesecake

Lemon Cake-Top Pudding

$^1/_4$ **cup sliced natural almonds**
4 **eggs, separated**
1 **cup sugar**
3 **tablespoons margarine, softened**
3 **tablespoons all-purpose flour**
$^1/_8$ **teaspoon salt**
$^1/_3$ **cup freshly squeezed SUNKIST® lemon juice**
1 **cup reduced-fat or lowfat milk**
Grated peel of $^1/_2$ SUNKIST® lemon

Preheat oven to 325°F. Spray the inside of $1^1/_2$-quart glass casserole with butter-flavored nonstick cooking spray. Sprinkle almonds over bottom of casserole. In medium bowl, with electric mixer, beat egg whites at high speed until soft peaks form. Gradually add $^1/_4$ cup sugar, beating until medium-stiff peaks form; set aside. With same beaters, in large bowl, beat together margarine and remaining $^3/_4$ cup sugar. With same beaters, in small bowl, beat egg yolks well; add to margarine-sugar mixture, beating thoroughly. Add flour, salt and lemon juice; beat well. Stir in milk and lemon peel until blended. Stir in $^1/_3$ of the egg white mixture, then gently fold in remaining egg whites. Pour batter into prepared casserole over almonds. Place casserole in shallow baking pan filled with 1 inch hot water. Bake, uncovered, for 50 to 55 minutes, or until golden brown and top springs back when lightly touched with finger. Carefully remove from water and let set for 20 to 30 minutes. Serve warm or chilled. Garnish each serving with lemon half-cartwheel slices and fresh mint leaves, if desired.

Makes 6 to 8 servings

Lemon Cake-Top Pudding

Toffee Bread Pudding with Cinnamon Toffee Sauce

    3 cups milk
    4 eggs
    ³/₄ cup sugar
    ³/₄ teaspoon ground cinnamon
    ³/₄ teaspoon vanilla extract
    ¹/₂ teaspoon salt
    6 to 6¹/₂ cups ¹/₂-inch cubes French, Italian or
        sourdough bread
    1 cup SKOR® English Toffee Bits or HEATH®
        BITS 'O BRICKLE® Almond Toffee Bits, divided
    Cinnamon Toffee Sauce (recipe follows)
    Sweetened whipped cream or ice cream (optional)

1. Heat oven to 350°F. Butter 13×9×2-inch baking pan.

2. Mix together milk, eggs, sugar, cinnamon, vanilla and salt in large bowl with wire whisk. Stir in bread cubes, coating completely. Allow to stand 10 minutes. Stir in ¹/₂ cup toffee bits. Pour into prepared pan. Sprinkle remaining ¹/₂ cup toffee bits over surface.

3. Bake 40 to 45 minutes or until surface is set. Cool 30 minutes.

4. Meanwhile, prepare Cinnamon Toffee Sauce. Cut pudding into squares; top with sauce and sweetened whipped cream or ice cream, if desired.

Makes 12 servings

Cinnamon Toffee Sauce: *Combine ³/₄ cup SKOR® English Toffee Bits or HEATH® BITS 'O BRICKLE® Almond Toffee Bits, ¹/₃ cup whipping cream and ¹/₈ teaspoon ground cinnamon in medium saucepan. Cook over low heat, stirring constantly, until toffee melts and mixture is well blended. (As toffee melts, small bits of almond will remain.) Makes about ²/₃ cup sauce.*

Note: *This dessert is best eaten the same day it is prepared.*

Toffee Bread Pudding with Cinnamon Toffee Sauce

Banana Pudding

60 to 70 vanilla wafers*
1 cup granulated sugar
3 tablespoons cornstarch
1/4 teaspoon salt
2 cans (12 fluid ounces each) NESTLÉ® CARNATION®
   Evaporated Milk
2 eggs, lightly beaten
3 tablespoons butter, cut into pieces
1 1/2 teaspoons vanilla extract
5 ripe but firm large bananas, cut into 1/4-inch slices
1 container (8 ounces) frozen whipped topping,
   thawed

*A 12-ounce box of vanilla wafers contains about 88 wafers.

LINE bottom and side of 2 1/2-quart glass bowl with about 40 wafers.

COMBINE sugar, cornstarch and salt in medium saucepan. Gradually stir in evaporated milk to dissolve cornstarch. Whisk in eggs. Add butter. Cook over medium heat, stirring constantly, until the mixture begins to thicken. Reduce heat to low; bring to a simmer and cook for 1 minute, stirring constantly. Remove from heat. Stir in vanilla extract. Let cool slightly.

POUR half of pudding over wafers. Top with half of bananas. Layer remaining vanilla wafers over bananas. Combine remaining pudding and bananas; spoon over wafers. Refrigerate for at least 4 hours. Top with whipped topping.   *Makes 8 servings*

Baked Apples

2 tablespoons sugar
2 tablespoons raisins, chopped
2 tablespoons chopped walnuts
2 tablespoons GRANDMA'S® Molasses
6 apples, cored

Heat oven to 350°F. In medium bowl, combine sugar, raisins, walnuts and molasses. Fill apple cavities with molasses mixture. Place in 13×9-inch baking dish. Pour ½ cup hot water over apples and bake 25 minutes or until soft.

Makes 6 servings

Strawberry Dessert

2 cups graham cracker crumbs
⅓ cup margarine, melted
¼ cup granulated sugar
2 packages (8 ounces each) cream cheese, softened
1 cup powdered sugar
2 containers (6 ounces each) lemon-flavor yogurt
3 pints strawberries, sliced
1 container (12 ounces) frozen whipped topping, thawed

1. Combine cracker crumbs, granulated sugar and margarine in medium bowl; mix well. Press into bottom of 13×9-inch baking dish.

2. Beat cream cheese and powdered sugar 1 minute in medium bowl with electric mixer at medium speed. Beat in yogurt until blended. Pour mixture over crust. Arrange strawberries on cream cheese mixture. Spread whipped topping over strawberries. Chill at least 4 hours or overnight before serving.

Makes 9 to 12 servings

Triple Chip Cheesecake

Crust
1³/₄ cups chocolate graham cracker crumbs
¹/₃ cup butter or margarine, melted

Filling
    3 packages (8 ounces each) cream cheese, softened
³/₄ cup granulated sugar
¹/₂ cup sour cream
    3 tablespoons all-purpose flour
1¹/₂ teaspoons vanilla extract
    3 eggs
    1 cup (6 ounces) NESTLÉ® TOLL HOUSE® Butterscotch
       Flavored Morsels
    1 cup (6 ounces) NESTLÉ® TOLL HOUSE® Semi-Sweet
       Chocolate Morsels
    1 cup (6 ounces) NESTLÉ® TOLL HOUSE® Premier
       White Morsels

Topping
    1 tablespoon each NESTLÉ® TOLL HOUSE®
       Butterscotch Flavored Morsels, Semi-Sweet
       Chocolate Morsels and Premier White Morsels

PREHEAT oven to 300°F. Grease 9-inch springform pan.

For Crust
COMBINE crumbs and butter in small bowl. Press onto bottom and 1 inch up side of prepared pan.

For Filling
BEAT cream cheese and granulated sugar in large mixer bowl until smooth. Add sour cream, flour and vanilla extract; mix well. Add eggs; beat on low speed until combined. Melt butterscotch morsels according to package directions. Stir until smooth. Add 1¹/₂ cups batter to melted morsels. Pour into crust. Repeat procedure with semi-sweet morsels. Carefully spoon over butterscotch layer. Melt Premier White morsels according to package directions and blend into remaining batter in mixer bowl. Carefully pour over semi-sweet layer.

continued on page 174

Triple Chip Cheesecake

Triple Chip Cheesecake, continued

BAKE *for 1 hour and 10 to 15 minutes or until center is almost set. Cool in pan on wire rack for 10 minutes. Run knife around edge of cheesecake. Let stand for 1 hour.*

For Topping
PLACE *each flavor of morsels separately into three small, heavy-duty resealable plastic food storage bags. Microwave on HIGH (100%) power for 20 seconds; knead bags to mix. Microwave at additional 10-second intervals, kneading until smooth. Cut small hole in corner of each bag; squeeze to drizzle over cheesecake. Refrigerate for at least 3 hours or overnight. Remove side of pan.* *Makes 12 to 16 servings*

Winter Fruit Compote

> 1 **can (16 ounces) pitted dark sweet cherries in syrup, undrained**
> 1 **teaspoon cornstarch**
> 1 **tablespoon almond-flavored liqueur or** $^1/_2$ **teaspoon almond extract**
> $1^1/_2$ **tablespoons honey**
> 2 **ripe Bartlett or Comice pears, peeled, cored and cut into 1-inch cubes**
> 1 **teaspoon chopped fresh mint**
> **Mint sprigs (optional)**

1. *Drain cherries reserving* $^1/_4$ *cup liquid. Combine reserved liquid and cornstarch in small bowl; mix until smooth. Add mixture to saucepan and bring to boil, over medium-high heat; stirring frequently. Reduce heat to simmer, as mixture begins to thicken, stir in liqueur and honey.*

2. *Stir in pears and drained cherries. Cook 2 minutes or until fruit is warm, stirring occasionally. Spoon into dessert dishes; sprinkle with mint and garnish with mint sprigs, if desired. Serve warm or at room temperature.* *Makes 4 servings*

Cookies and Cream Layered Dessert

1 cup cold milk
1 package (4-serving size) white chocolate-flavored
    instant pudding mix
1 package chocolate creme-filled sandwich cookies
1/4 cup butter, melted
2 packages (8 ounces each) cream cheese, softened
2 cups powdered sugar
1 container (8 ounces) frozen whipped topping,
    thawed
1 teaspoon vanilla
2 cups whipping cream

1. Combine milk and pudding mix in medium bowl; beat with wire whisk. (Pudding will be thick.) Set aside.

2. Finely crush cookies in resealable plastic food storage bag with rolling pin or in blender. Combine 2 cups crushed cookies and butter in small bowl. Place on bottom of 2-quart trifle dish. Reserve remaining crushed cookies.

3. Beat cream cheese and powdered sugar 2 minutes in large bowl with electric mixer at medium speed until blended. Fold in pudding mixture, whipped topping and vanilla.

4. Beat whipping cream in small deep bowl with electric mixer until soft peaks form. Fold into cream cheese mixture.

5. Spoon 1/3 cream cheese mixture over crushed cookies. Sprinkle 1/3 of remaining cookie crumbs over cream cheese layer. Repeat layers twice using remaining cream cheese mixture and cookie crumbs. Refrigerate until ready to serve.   Makes 12 servings

Lemon Cheesecake

Crust
- 35 vanilla wafers
- $^3/_4$ cup slivered almonds, toasted
- $^1/_3$ cup sugar
- $^1/_4$ cup butter, melted

Filling
- 3 packages (8 ounces each) cream cheese, softened
- $^3/_4$ cup sugar
- 4 eggs
- $^1/_3$ cup whipping cream
- $^1/_4$ cup lemon juice
- 1 tablespoon grated lemon peel
- 1 teaspoon vanilla

Topping
- 1 pint strawberries
- 2 tablespoons sugar

1. Preheat oven to 375°F. For crust, combine wafers, almonds and $^1/_3$ cup sugar in food processor; process until fine crumbs are formed. Combine crumb mixture with melted butter in medium bowl. Press mixture evenly on bottom and 1 inch up side of 9-inch springform pan. Set aside.

2. For filling, beat cream cheese and $^3/_4$ cup sugar in large bowl at high speed of electric mixer 2 to 3 minutes or until fluffy. Add eggs one at a time, beating after each addition. Add whipping cream, lemon juice, lemon peel and vanilla; beat just until blended. Pour into prepared crust. Place springform pan on baking sheet. Bake 45 to 55 minutes or until set. Cool completely on wire rack. Cover and refrigerate at least 10 hours or overnight.

3. To complete recipe, for topping, hull and slice strawberries. Combine with sugar in medium bowl. Let stand 15 minutes. Serve over cheesecake.

Makes 16 servings

Make-ahead time: 10 hours or overnight
Final prep/stand time: 20 minutes

Lemon Cheesecake

Plum Streusel

Plum Filling
- $1/2$ **cup firmly packed light brown sugar**
- 3 **tablespoons cornstarch**
- $1/2$ **teaspoon ground nutmeg**
- $2^1/2$ **pounds ripe plums, pitted and sliced $1/2$ inch thick**

Streusel
- 1 **cup all-purpose flour**
- $1/2$ **Butter Flavor CRISCO® Stick or $1/2$ cup Butter Flavor CRISCO® all-vegetable shortening**
- $1/2$ **cup firmly packed light brown sugar**
- 1 **teaspoon ground cinnamon**
- 1 **teaspoon vanilla**
- $1/4$ **teaspoon salt**

1. *Heat oven to 350°F. Spray 3-quart shallow baking dish with CRISCO® No-Stick Cooking Spray; set aside.*

2. *For filling, combine brown sugar, cornstarch and nutmeg in large bowl; mix well. Add plums and stir gently to coat evenly. Place in prepared pan.*

3. *For streusel, combine flour, $1/2$ cup shortening, $1/2$ cup brown sugar, cinnamon, vanilla and salt in large bowl. Mix with fork until mixture is combined and just crumbly. Do not overmix. Sprinkle over fruit mixture.*

4. *Bake at 350°F for 45 minutes or until streusel top is crisp. Cool about 10 minutes; serve warm with whipped cream or ice cream.*

Makes 6 to 8 servings

Tip: *Streusel is the German word for "sprinkle" and that is exactly how you're going to add the topping. This easy dessert is perfect for summer holiday entertaining.*

Plum Streusel

Double Almond Ice Cream

            3 cups whipping cream
            1 cup milk
        3/4 cup plus 2 tablespoons sugar, divided
            4 egg yolks, beaten
            1 tablespoon vanilla extract
            2 teaspoons almond extract
            2 tablespoons butter
        1 1/2 cups BLUE DIAMOND® Chopped Natural Almonds

Combine cream, milk and 3/4 cup sugar in medium saucepan. Cook and stir over medium heat until sugar is dissolved and mixture is hot. Gradually add 1 cup cream mixture to beaten egg yolks, whisking constantly. When mixture is smooth, strain into double boiler. Gradually pour in remaining cream mixture, whisking constantly. Cook over simmering water until mixture thickens slightly and coats back of spoon, about 8 minutes, stirring constantly. Do not boil. Stir in extracts. Cool.

Meanwhile, melt butter in small saucepan; stir in remaining 2 tablespoons sugar. Cook and stir over medium heat until sugar begins to bubble, about 30 seconds. Add almonds; cook and stir over medium heat until golden and well coated. Cool. Stir almonds into ice cream mixture. Pour into ice cream maker container. Freeze according to manufacturer's instructions.

Makes 1 quart ice cream

Tip: Do not add eggs or egg yolks to a hot liquid. Instead stir a small amount of the hot liquid into the egg, then add the egg mixture to the hot liquid. Be careful not to allow the egg mixture to boil.

Double Almond Ice Cream

Baked Apple Slices with Peanut Butter Crumble

4 cups peeled and thinly sliced apples
1 cup sugar, divided
1 cup all-purpose flour, divided
3 tablespoons butter or margarine, divided
1 cup quick-cooking or old-fashioned rolled oats
1/2 teaspoon ground cinnamon
1 cup REESE'S® Creamy or Crunchy Peanut Butter
Sweetened whipped cream or ice cream (optional)

1. Heat oven to 350°F. Grease 9-inch square baking pan.

2. Stir together apples, 3/4 cup sugar and 1/4 cup flour in large bowl. Spread in prepared pan; dot with 2 tablespoons butter. Combine oats, remaining 3/4 cup flour, remaining 1/4 cup sugar and cinnamon in medium bowl; set aside.

3. Place remaining 1 tablespoon butter and peanut butter in small microwave-safe bowl. Microwave at HIGH (100%) 30 seconds or until butter is melted; stir until smooth. Add to oat mixture; blend until crumbs are formed. Sprinkle crumb mixture over apples.

4. Bake 40 to 45 minutes or until apples are tender and edges are bubbly. Cool slightly. Serve warm or cool with whipped cream or ice cream, if desired.

Makes 6 to 8 servings

Baked Apple Slices with Peanut Butter Crumble

Berry Cobbler

1 pint (2¹/₂ cups) fresh raspberries*
1 pint (2¹/₂ cups) fresh blueberries or strawberries,*
    sliced
2 tablespoons cornstarch
¹/₂ to ³/₄ cup sugar
1 cup all-purpose flour
1¹/₂ teaspoons baking powder
¹/₄ teaspoon salt
¹/₃ cup milk
¹/₃ cup butter or margarine, melted
2 tablespoons thawed frozen apple juice concentrate
¹/₄ teaspoon ground nutmeg

One (16-ounce) bag frozen raspberries and one (16-ounce) bag frozen blueberries or strawberries can be substituted for fresh berries. Thaw berries, reserving juices. Increase cornstarch to 3 tablespoons.

1. Preheat oven to 375°F.

2. Combine berries and cornstarch in medium bowl; toss lightly to coat. Add sugar to taste; mix well. Spoon into 1¹/₂-quart or 8-inch square baking dish. Combine flour, baking powder and salt in medium bowl. Add milk, butter and juice concentrate; mix just until dry ingredients are moistened. Drop 6 heaping tablespoonfuls batter evenly over berries; sprinkle with nutmeg.

3. Bake 25 minutes or until topping is golden brown and fruit is bubbly. Cool on wire rack. Serve warm or at room temperature.

Makes 6 servings

Tip: Cobblers are best served warm or at room temperature on the day they are made. Leftovers should be kept covered and refrigerated for up to two days. Reheat them, covered, in a 350°F oven until warm.

Prep Time: 5 minutes
Bake Time: 25 minutes

Classic Rice Pudding

1 (14-ounce) can EAGLE BRAND® Sweetened
    Condensed Milk (NOT evaporated milk)
2 egg yolks
$1/4$ cup water
$1/2$ teaspoon ground cinnamon
2 cups uncooked long grain rice, cooked
$1/2$ cup raisins
2 teaspoons vanilla extract
    Additional ground cinnamon

1. In large saucepan, combine Eagle Brand, egg yolks, water and cinnamon. Over medium heat, cook and stir 10 to 15 minutes or until mixture thickens slightly.

2. Remove from heat; add cooked rice, raisins and vanilla. Cool. Chill thoroughly. Sprinkle with additional cinnamon. Refrigerate leftovers.

Makes 8 to 10 servings

Ambrosia

1 can (20 ounces) DOLE® Pineapple Chunks, drained
1 can (11 or 15 ounces) DOLE® Mandarin Oranges,
    drained
1 DOLE® Banana, sliced
$1^{1}/2$ cups seedless grapes
$1/2$ cup miniature marshmallows
1 cup vanilla lowfat yogurt
$1/4$ cup flaked coconut, toasted

• Combine pineapple chunks, mandarin oranges, banana, grapes and marshmallows in medium bowl.

• Stir yogurt into fruit mixture. Sprinkle with coconut.

Makes 4 to 6 servings

Prep Time: *15 minutes*

Cookies and Brownies

Layered Cookie Bars

$^3/_4$ cup (1$^1/_2$ sticks) butter or margarine
1$^3/_4$ cups vanilla wafer crumbs
6 tablespoons HERSHEY'S Cocoa
$^1/_4$ cup sugar
1 can (14 ounces) sweetened condensed milk
1 cup HERSHEY'S Semi-Sweet Chocolate Chips
$^3/_4$ cup SKOR® English Toffee Bits
1 cup chopped walnuts

1. Heat oven to 350°F. Melt butter in 13×9×2-inch baking pan in oven. Combine crumbs, cocoa and sugar; sprinkle over butter.

2. Pour sweetened condensed milk evenly on top of crumbs. Top with chocolate chips and toffee bits, then nuts; press down firmly.

3. Bake 25 to 30 minutes or until lightly browned. Cool completely in pan on wire rack. Chill, if desired. Cut into bars. Store covered at room temperature.

Makes about 36 bars

Layered Cookie Bars

Pumpkin Spiced and Iced Cookies

2^1/$_4$ cups all-purpose flour
1^1/$_2$ teaspoons pumpkin pie spice
1 teaspoon baking powder
^{1}/$_2$ teaspoon baking soda
^{1}/$_2$ teaspoon salt
1 cup (2 sticks) butter or margarine, softened
1 cup granulated sugar
1 can (15 ounces) LIBBY'S® 100% Pure Pumpkin
2 eggs
1 teaspoon vanilla extract
2 cups (12-ounce package) NESTLÉ® TOLL HOUSE®
   Semi-Sweet Chocolate Morsels
1 cup chopped walnuts (optional)
Vanilla Glaze (recipe follows)

PREHEAT oven to 375°F. Grease baking sheets.

COMBINE flour, pumpkin pie spice, baking powder, baking soda and salt in medium bowl. Beat butter and granulated sugar in large mixer bowl until creamy. Beat in pumpkin, eggs and vanilla extract. Gradually beat in flour mixture. Stir in morsels and nuts. Drop by rounded tablespoon onto prepared baking sheets.

BAKE for 15 to 20 minutes or until edges are lightly browned. Cool on baking sheets for 2 minutes; remove to wire rack to cool completely. Spread or drizzle with Vanilla Glaze.   *Makes about 5^1/$_2$ dozen cookies*

Vanilla Glaze: **COMBINE** 1 cup powdered sugar, 1 to 1^1/$_2$ tablespoons milk and ^{1}/$_2$ teaspoon vanilla extract in small bowl; mix well.

Pumpkin Spiced and Iced Cookies

Brownie Quilt Cake

1 **package (about 18 ounces) brownie mix, plus
    ingredients to prepare mix**
1 **container (16 ounces) vanilla frosting**
1 **tube (4¼ ounces) chocolate decorator icing
    Assorted colored sugars
    Ribbon (optional)**

1. Prepare brownie mix according to package directions and bake in 8-inch square baking pan. Cool in pan on wire rack 10 to 15 minutes. Run knife around edges to loosen. Remove from pan and invert brownie onto wire rack. Cool completely.

2. Transfer brownie to serving plate. Frost top with vanilla frosting. Place chocolate decorator icing in small resealable plastic food storage bag and seal. With scissors, snip off one corner of bag. Gently squeeze bag to pipe quilt pattern on brownie. Fill in quilt pattern with colored sugars. Wrap edge with ribbon, if desired.   *Makes 8 servings*

Note: For a large celebration, make four brownie quilts and place them together as an unusual and attention-getting edible centerpiece. Pipe a wide strip of chocolate frosting to "connect" the four quilts into one large quilt. Wrap all 4 quilts with one long ribbon.

Tip: For this cake, choose a brownie mix meant to be baked in a 8- or 9-inch square pan.

Brownie Quilt Cake

Chocolate Peanut Butter Shortbread Bars

Chocolate Shortbread
  1 cup butter, softened
  $^{3}/_{4}$ cup sugar
  $^{1}/_{3}$ cup unsweetened cocoa
  1 teaspoon vanilla extract
  2 cups all-purpose flour

Peanut Butter Layer
  1 cup butter, softened
  1 cup sugar
  $^{1}/_{4}$ cup crunchy peanut butter
  1 egg yolk
  1 teaspoon vanilla extract
  $1^{1}/_{3}$ cups all-purpose flour
  1 cup rolled oats

Garnish
  $^{1}/_{2}$ cup dry-roasted peanuts, finely chopped

Preheat oven to 300°F.

To make chocolate shortbread: In a bowl, cream together the butter, sugar, cocoa and vanilla. Mix in the flour until smooth. Set aside.

To make the peanut butter layer: Cream together the butter, sugar and peanut butter. Add the egg yolk and vanilla. Mix in the flour and oats.

Grease a 13×9-inch baking dish. Pat half of the chocolate shortbread into the pan. (This will be a thin layer.) Spread the peanut butter layer over the chocolate layer. Carefully pat the remaining shortbread dough evenly over the peanut butter layer to cover completely. Gently pat peanuts into the shortbread.

Bake for about 1 hour, checking after 45 minutes. The shortbread will be done when the sides look dry. Cut into squares while still hot. Let the shortbread cool before removing it from the pan.   *Makes 32 bars*

Favorite recipe from **Texas Peanut Producers Board**

Chocolate Peanut Butter Shortbread Bars

Apple Crisp Cookies

Cookies

1 Butter Flavor CRISCO® Stick or 1 cup Butter Flavor
  CRISCO® all-vegetable shortening plus additional
  for greasing
1 cup firmly packed light brown sugar
1 teaspoon vanilla
2¹/₂ cups oats (quick or old-fashioned, uncooked)
2¹/₄ cups all-purpose flour
¹/₂ teaspoon baking soda
¹/₂ teaspoon salt
6 to 8 tablespoons water

Topping

1 can (21 ounces) apple pie filling, finely chopped
1 cup reserved crumb mixture
¹/₂ cup finely chopped pecans or walnuts

1. Heat oven to 375°F. Grease baking sheet with shortening. Place sheets of foil on countertop for cooling cookies.

2. For cookies, combine 1 cup shortening, brown sugar and vanilla in large bowl. Beat at medium speed of electric mixer until well blended.

3. Combine oats, flour, baking soda and salt. Add alternately with water to creamed mixture stirring with spoon. Mix well after each addition. (Mixture will be crumbly, but will hold together when shaped into small ball.) Add additional water if necessary. Reserve 1 cup for topping. Shape remaining dough into 1-inch balls. Place 2 inches apart on greased baking sheet. Flatten to ¹/₈-inch thickness with floured bottom of glass. Smooth edges.

4. Bake at 375°F for 5 to 7 minutes or until light brown around edges and firm. Do not overbake. Remove from oven. Cool on baking sheet about 5 minutes.

5. For topping, place 1 measuring teaspoonful of pie filling in center of each cookie. Spread carefully to cover.

continued on page 196

Apple Crisp Cookies

Apple Crisp Cookies, continued

6. Combine 1 cup reserved crumbs and nuts in small bowl. Toss until mixed. Sprinkle over apple filling.

7. Return to oven. Bake 5 minutes or until topping is light brown. Do not overbake. Cool 2 minutes on baking sheet. Remove cookies to foil to cool completely.   *Makes about 3 dozen cookies*

Luscious Fresh Lemon Bars

Crust
$^1/_2$ **cup butter or margarine, softened**
$^1/_2$ **cup granulated sugar**
    Grated peel of $^1/_2$ SUNKIST® lemon
$1^1/_4$ **cups all-purpose flour**

Lemon Layer
4 **eggs**
$1^2/_3$ **cups granulated sugar**
3 **tablespoons all-purpose flour**
$^1/_2$ **teaspoon baking powder**
    Grated peel of $^1/_2$ SUNKIST® lemon
    Juice of 2 SUNKIST® lemons (6 tablespoons)
1 **teaspoon vanilla extract**
    Confectioners' sugar

To make crust, in bowl blend together butter, granulated sugar and lemon peel. Gradually stir in flour to form a soft crumbly dough. Press evenly into bottom of foil-lined 13×9×2-inch baking pan. Bake at 350°F for 15 minutes.

Meanwhile, to prepare lemon layer, in large bowl whisk or beat eggs well. Stir together granulated sugar, flour and baking powder. Gradually whisk sugar mixture into beaten eggs. Stir or whisk in lemon peel, lemon juice and vanilla. Pour over hot baked crust. Return to oven and bake for 20 to 25 minutes, or until top and sides are lightly browned. Cool. Using foil on two sides, lift out the cookie base and gently loosen foil along all sides. With a long wet knife, cut into bars or squares. Sprinkle tops with confectioners' sugar.   *Makes about 3 dozen bars*

Dad's Ginger Molasses Cookies

1 cup shortening
1 cup granulated sugar
1 tablespoon baking soda
2 teaspoons ground ginger
2 teaspoons ground cinnamon
1 teaspoon ground cloves
$^1\!/_2$ teaspoon salt
1 cup molasses
$^2\!/_3$ cup double-strength instant coffee *
1 egg
4$^3\!/_4$ cups all-purpose flour

*To prepare double-strength coffee, follow instructions for instant coffee but use twice the recommended amount of instant coffee granules.

1. Preheat oven to 350°F. Lightly grease cookie sheets.

2. Beat shortening and sugar with electric mixer until creamy. Beat in baking soda, ginger, cinnamon, cloves and salt until well blended. Add molasses, coffee and egg, one at a time, beating well after each addition. Gradually add flour, beating on low speed just until blended.

3. Drop dough by rounded tablespoonfuls 2 inches apart on prepared cookie sheets. Bake 12 to 15 minutes or until cookies are set but not browned. Cool on cookie sheets 1 minute. Remove to wire racks; cool completely.

Makes about 6 dozen cookies

Rocky Road Brownies

1 cup miniature marshmallows
1¼ cups HERSHEY'S Semi-Sweet Chocolate Chips
½ cup chopped nuts
½ cup (1 stick) butter or margarine
1 cup sugar
2 eggs
1 teaspoon vanilla extract
½ cup all-purpose flour
⅓ cup HERSHEY'S Cocoa
½ teaspoon baking powder
½ teaspoon salt

1. Heat oven to 350°F. Grease 9-inch square baking pan.

2. Stir together marshmallows, chocolate chips and nuts; set aside. Place butter in large microwave-safe bowl. Microwave at HIGH (100% power) 1 to 1½ minutes or until melted. Add sugar, eggs and vanilla, beating with spoon until well blended. Add flour, cocoa, baking powder and salt; blend well. Spread batter in prepared pan.

3. Bake 22 minutes. Sprinkle chocolate chip mixture over top. Continue baking 5 minutes or until marshmallows have softened and puffed slightly. Cool completely. With wet knife, cut into squares.

Makes about 20 brownies

Rocky Road Brownies

Mincemeat Oatmeal Cookies

$^1/_2$ **Butter Flavor CRISCO® Stick or $^1/_2$ cup Butter
Flavor CRISCO® all-vegetable shortening**
1 **cup firmly packed brown sugar**
1 **egg**
$1^1/_3$ **cups prepared mincemeat**
$1^1/_2$ **cups all-purpose flour**
1 **teaspoon baking soda**
$^1/_2$ **teaspoon salt**
1 **cup quick oats (not instant or old-fashioned)**
$^1/_2$ **cup coarsely chopped walnuts**

1. Heat oven to 350°F. Grease baking sheet with shortening. Place sheets of foil on countertop for cooling cookies.

2. Combine $^1/_2$ cup shortening, sugar and egg in large bowl. Beat at medium speed of electric mixer until well blended. Beat in mincemeat.

3. Combine flour, baking soda and salt. Mix into creamed mixture at low speed until blended. Stir in oats and nuts with spoon.

4. Drop rounded tablespoonfuls of dough 2 inches apart onto prepared baking sheet.

5. Bake at 350°F for 12 minutes, or until set and lightly browned around edges. Do not overbake. Cool 2 minutes on baking sheet. Remove cookies to foil to cool completely.   Makes about 5 dozen cookies

Tip: While mincemeat once contained meat, it is now a spicy mixture of apples, pears, raisins and other fruits. Look for it in the baking section of your supermarket.

Mincemeat Oatmeal Cookies

Peanutty Gooey Bars

Crust
  2 cups chocolate graham cracker crumbs
  ¹/₂ cup (1 stick) butter or margarine, melted
  ¹/₃ cup granulated sugar

Topping
  1²/₃ cups (11-ounce package) NESTLÉ® TOLL HOUSE®
      Peanut Butter & Milk Chocolate Morsels, divided
  1 can (14 ounces) NESTLÉ® CARNATION® Sweetened
      Condensed Milk
  1 teaspoon vanilla extract
  1 cup coarsely chopped peanuts

PREHEAT *oven to 350°F.*

For Crust
COMBINE *graham cracker crumbs, butter and sugar in medium bowl; press onto bottom of ungreased 13×9-inch baking pan.*

For Topping
MICROWAVE *1 cup morsels, sweetened condensed milk and vanilla extract in medium, uncovered, microwave-safe bowl on HIGH (100%) power for 1 minute. Stir. Morsels may retain some of their original shape. If necessary, microwave at additional 10- to 15-second intervals, stirring until morsels are melted. Pour evenly over crust. Top with nuts and remaining morsels.*

BAKE *for 20 to 25 minutes or until edges are bubbly. Cool completely in pan on wire rack. Cut into bars.*   *Makes 2 dozen bars*

Peanutty Gooey Bars

Pfeffernüsse

3¹/₂ **cups all-purpose flour**
2 **teaspoons baking powder**
1¹/₂ **teaspoons ground cinnamon**
1 **teaspoon ground ginger**
¹/₂ **teaspoon baking soda**
¹/₂ **teaspoon salt**
¹/₂ **teaspoon ground cloves**
¹/₂ **teaspoon ground cardamom**
¹/₄ **teaspoon black pepper**
1 **cup butter, softened**
1 **cup granulated sugar**
¹/₄ **cup dark molasses**
1 **egg**
Powdered sugar

1. *Combine flour, baking powder, cinnamon, ginger, baking soda, salt, cloves, cardamom and pepper in large bowl.*

2. *Beat butter and sugar in large bowl with electric mixer at medium speed until light and fluffy. Beat in molasses and egg. Gradually add flour mixture. Beat at low speed until dough forms. Shape dough into disk; wrap in plastic wrap and refrigerate until firm, 30 minutes or up to 3 days.*

3. *Preheat oven to 350°F. Grease cookie sheets. Roll dough into 1-inch balls. Place 2 inches apart on prepared cookie sheets.*

4. *Bake 12 to 14 minutes or until golden brown. Transfer cookies to wire racks; dust with sifted powdered sugar. Cool completely. Store tightly covered at room temperature or freeze up to 3 months.*

Makes about 5 dozen cookies

Cheesecake Marble Brownies

6 squares (1 ounce each) semi-sweet chocolate
³/₄ cup (1¹/₂ sticks) IMPERIAL® Spread, softened, divided
1³/₄ cups all-purpose flour, divided
1 teaspoon baking powder
¹/₂ teaspoon salt
2 cups sugar, divided
4 eggs, divided
1¹/₂ teaspoons vanilla extract, divided
1 package (8 ounces) cream cheese, softened

Preheat oven to 350°F. Grease 13×9-inch baking pan; set aside.

In medium saucepan, melt chocolate with ¹/₂ cup Imperial Spread over low heat, stirring occasionally. Remove from heat and let cool slightly. In medium bowl, blend 1¹/₂ cups flour, baking powder and salt; set aside.

In medium bowl, with wire whisk, beat 1¹/₄ cups sugar, 3 eggs and ¹/₂ teaspoon vanilla. Stir egg mixture, then flour mixture, into cooled chocolate mixture. Spread into prepared pan.

In medium bowl, with electric mixer, beat cream cheese, remaining ³/₄ cup sugar and ¹/₄ cup Imperial Spread until smooth. Beat in remaining egg and 1 teaspoon vanilla, then remaining ¹/₄ cup flour. Spoon over chocolate batter and gently spread in even layer. With tip of knife, gently marble in cream cheese mixture.

Bake 30 minutes or until set. On wire rack, cool completely. To serve, cut into bars. *Makes 24 brownies*

Lemon Coconut Pixies

¼ cup (½ stick) butter or margarine, softened
1 cup sugar
2 eggs
1½ teaspoons freshly grated lemon peel
1½ cups all-purpose flour
2 teaspoons baking powder
¼ teaspoon salt
1 cup MOUNDS™ Sweetened Coconut Flakes
Powdered sugar

1. *Heat oven to 300°F.*

2. *Beat butter, sugar, eggs and lemon peel in large bowl until well blended. Stir together flour, baking powder and salt; gradually add to lemon mixture, beating until blended. Stir in coconut. Cover; refrigerate dough about 1 hour or until firm enough to handle. Shape into 1-inch balls; roll in powdered sugar. Place 2 inches apart on ungreased cookie sheet.*

3. *Bake 15 to 18 minutes or until edges are set. Immediately remove from cookie sheet to wire rack. Cool completely. Store in tightly covered container in cool, dry place.* *Makes about 4 dozen cookies*

Lemon Coconut Pixies

Snickerdoodles

2 cups sugar, divided
1 Butter Flavor CRISCO® Stick or 1 cup Butter Flavor
   CRISCO® all-vegetable shortening
2 eggs
2 tablespoons milk
1 teaspoon vanilla
2¾ cups all-purpose flour
2 teaspoons cream of tartar
1 teaspoon baking soda
¾ teaspoon salt
2 teaspoons ground cinnamon

1. Heat oven to 400°F. Place sheets of foil on countertop for cooling cookies.

2. Combine 1½ cups sugar, 1 cup shortening, eggs, milk and vanilla in large bowl. Beat at medium speed of electric mixer until well blended.

3. Combine flour, cream of tartar, baking soda and salt. Add gradually to creamed mixture at low speed. Mix just until blended. Shape dough into 1-inch balls.

4. Combine remaining ½ cup sugar and cinnamon in small bowl. Roll balls of dough in mixture. Place 2 inches apart on ungreased baking sheet.

5. Bake for 7 to 8 minutes. Do not overbake. Cool 2 minutes on baking sheet. Remove cookies to foil to cool completely.   *Makes 6 dozen cookies*

Hint: Cinnamon-sugar mixture can be put in resealable plastic bag. Place 2 to 3 dough balls at a time in bag. Seal. Shake to sugar-coat dough.

Colored Sugar Snickerdoodles: Add 2 teaspoons cinnamon to flour mixture in Step 3. Combine 3 tablespoons colored sugar and 3 tablespoons granulated sugar. Use for coating instead of cinnamon-sugar mixture.

Spiced Raisin Cookies with White Chocolate Drizzle

2 cups all-purpose flour
1 teaspoon baking soda
1¹/₂ teaspoons ground cinnamon
1 teaspoon ground ginger
¹/₂ teaspoon ground allspice
¹/₄ teaspoon salt
³/₄ cup butter, softened
1 cup sugar
¹/₄ cup molasses
1 egg
1 cup SUN-MAID® Raisins or Golden Raisins
4 ounces white chocolate, coarsely chopped

HEAT oven to 375°F.

COMBINE flour, baking soda, cinnamon, ginger, allspice and salt in a small bowl. Set aside.

BEAT butter and sugar until light and fluffy.

ADD molasses and egg; beat well.

BEAT in raisins. Gradually beat in flour mixture on low speed just until incorporated.

DROP dough by tablespoonfuls onto ungreased cookie sheets 2 inches apart. Flatten dough slightly.

BAKE 12 to 14 minutes or until set. Cool on cookie sheets 1 minute; transfer to wire rack and cool completely.

MICROWAVE chocolate in a heavy, resealable plastic bag at high power 30 seconds. Turn bag over; heat additional 30 to 45 seconds or until almost melted. Knead bag with hands to melt remaining chocolate. Cut a ¹/₈-inch corner off one end of bag. Drizzle cooled cookies with chocolate. Let stand until chocolate is set, about 20 minutes.   *Makes about 2 dozen cookies*

Prep Time: 15 minutes
Baking Time: 14 minutes

Hershey's Soft & Chewy Cookies

1 cup (2 sticks) butter (no substitutes)
3/4 cup packed light brown sugar
1/2 cup granulated sugar
1/4 cup light corn syrup
1 egg
2 teaspoons vanilla extract
2 1/2 cups all-purpose flour
1 teaspoon baking soda
1/4 teaspoon salt
1 package (10 to 12 ounces) HERSHEY'S Chips or
  Baking Bits (any flavor)

1. Heat oven to 350°F.

2. Beat butter, brown sugar and granulated sugar in large bowl until fluffy. Add corn syrup, egg and vanilla; beat well. Stir together flour, baking soda and salt; gradually add to butter mixture, beating until well blended. Stir in chips or bits. Drop by rounded teaspoons onto ungreased cookie sheet.

3. Bake 8 to 10 minutes or until lightly browned and almost set. Cool slightly; remove from cookie sheet to wire rack. Cool completely. Cookies will be softer the second day.   *Makes about 3 1/2 dozen cookies*

Chocolate Chocolate Cookies: Decrease flour to 2 1/4 cups and add 1/4 cup HERSHEY'S Cocoa or HERSHEY'S Dutch Processed Cocoa.

Hershey's Soft & Chewy Cookies

Snow~on~the~Mountain Cookies

Cookies
1¼ **Butter Flavor CRISCO® Sticks or 1¼ cups Butter Flavor CRISCO® all-vegetable shortening**
1 **cup sugar**
2 **eggs**
1 **tablespoon vanilla**
4 **cups all-purpose flour**
1 **teaspoon salt**
2 **cups (12-ounce package) semisweet chocolate chips**
1 **cup chopped walnuts**

Glaze
1⅔ **cups (10-ounce package) vanilla milk chips**
2 **to 5 tablespoons whipping cream or 1 to 3 tablespoons milk**

1. *Heat oven to 325°F. Place sheets of foil on countertop for cooling cookies.*

2. *For cookies, combine 1¼ cups shortening and sugar in large bowl. Beat at medium speed of electric mixer until well blended. Beat in eggs and vanilla.*

3. *Combine flour and salt. Add gradually to creamed mixture at low speed. Beat until well blended. Stir in chocolate chips and nuts with spoon. Shape dough into 1-inch balls. Shape top of ball into cone or mountain shape. Place 1 inch apart on ungreased baking sheet.*

4. *Bake at 325°F for 10 to 12 minutes or until light golden brown around bottom edge. Do not overbake. Cool on baking sheet 2 minutes. Remove cookies to foil to cool completely.*

5. *For glaze (prepare while cookies are baking), soften vanilla milk chips (see Melting/Drizzling Procedure, page 214). Add enough whipping cream to make medium glaze. Heat and stir until smooth. Spoon 1 teaspoonful over top of each warm cookie. Cool completely.* *Makes about 6 dozen cookies*

continued on page 214

Snow-on-the-Mountain Cookies

Snow-on-the-Mountain Cookies, continued

Melting/Drizzling Procedure: *For melting or drizzling, choose one of these easy methods. Start with chips and Butter Flavor Crisco® all-vegetable shortening (if called for), then: place in small microwave-safe measuring cup or bowl. Microwave at 50% (MEDIUM). Stir after 1 minute. Repeat until smooth. Drizzle from tip of spoon. **Or,** place in heavy resealable plastic sandwich bag. Seal. Microwave at 50% (MEDIUM). Check every minute until melted. Knead bag until smooth. Cut tiny tip off corner of bag. Squeeze out to drizzle. **Or,** place in small saucepan. Melt on range top on very low heat. Stir until smooth. Drizzle from tip of spoon.*

Oatmeal Hermits

3 cups QUAKER® Oats (quick or old fashioned, uncooked)
1 cup all-purpose flour
1 cup (2 sticks) butter or margarine, melted
1 cup firmly packed brown sugar
1 cup raisins
½ cup chopped nuts
1 egg
¼ cup milk
1 teaspoon ground cinnamon
1 teaspoon vanilla
½ teaspoon baking soda
½ teaspoon salt (optional)
¼ teaspoon ground nutmeg

Heat oven to 375°F. In large bowl, combine all ingredients; mix well. Drop by rounded tablespoonfuls onto ungreased cookie sheets. Bake 8 to 10 minutes. Cool 1 minute on cookie sheets; remove to wire cooling racks.

Makes about 3 dozen

For Bar Cookies: *Press dough into ungreased 15×10-inch jelly-roll pan. Bake about 17 minutes or until golden brown. Cool completely; cut into bars.*

The "Ultimate" Peanut Butter Whoopie Pie

Pies

$^1/_2$ Butter Flavor CRISCO® Stick or $^1/_2$ cup Butter Flavor CRISCO® all-vegetable shortening plus additional for greasing
1 cup milk
1 tablespoon white vinegar
1 cup granulated sugar
1 cup firmly packed brown sugar
$^3/_4$ cup JIF® Crunchy Peanut Butter
1 cup boiling water
1 teaspoon vanilla
4 cups all-purpose flour
$^1/_2$ cup unsweetened cocoa powder
2 teaspoons baking soda
$^1/_2$ teaspoon baking powder
$^1/_2$ teaspoon salt

Filling

$^1/_2$ cup milk
3 tablespoons all-purpose flour
2 cups confectioners' sugar
$^1/_2$ Butter Flavor CRISCO® Stick or $^1/_2$ cup Butter Flavor CRISCO® all-vegetable shortening
$^1/_2$ cup JIF® Creamy Peanut Butter
1 teaspoon vanilla

1. Heat oven to 425°F. Grease baking sheet with shortening. Place sheets of foil on countertop for cooling pies.

2. For cookies, combine 1 cup milk and vinegar in small microwavable bowl. Microwave at HIGH to warm slightly (or on rangetop in small saucepan on medium heat). Mixture will appear separated and curdled.

3. Combine granulated sugar, brown sugar and crunchy peanut butter in large bowl. Beat at medium speed with electric mixer until crumbly.

continued on page 216

The "Ultimate" Peanut Butter Whoopie Pie, continued

4. *Combine ½ cup shortening and boiling water. Stir to melt shortening. Add to peanut butter mixture along with milk mixture and vanilla. Beat at low speed. Mixture will be very fluid and somewhat separated.*

5. *Combine 4 cups flour, cocoa, baking soda, baking powder and salt. Stir well. Add all at once to peanut butter mixture. Beat at low speed until mixture is blended and resembles thick cake batter. Let stand 20 minutes. Drop by rounded measuring tablespoonfuls 2 inches apart onto prepared baking sheet.*

6. *Bake in upper half of oven for 8 to 10 minutes or until set. Do not overbake. Cool 2 minutes on baking sheet. Remove pies to foil to cool completely.*

7. *For filling, combine ½ cup milk and 3 tablespoons flour in small saucepan. Cook and stir on medium heat until thickened. Cool completely. Add confectioners' sugar, ½ cup shortening, creamy peanut butter and vanilla. Beat at low speed until blended. Beat at high until smooth. Refrigerate until ready to use. Spread filling on bottoms of half of the pies. Top with remaining halves. Press together gently.*

Makes 2½ dozen whoopie pies

The publisher would like to thank the companies and organizations listed below for the use of their recipes and photographs in this publication.

Blue Diamond Growers®

Bob Evans®

California Poultry Federation

Cherry Marketing Institute

Colorado Potato Administrative Committee

Del Monte Corporation

Dole Food Company, Inc.

Duncan Hines® and Moist Deluxe® are registered trademarks of Aurora Foods Inc.

Eagle Brand®

The Golden Grain Company®

Grandma's® is a registered trademark of Mott's, LLP

Hershey Foods Corporation

The Hidden Valley® Food Products Company

Hillshire Farm®

Hormel Foods, LLC

Lawry's® Foods

MASTERFOODS USA

Mrs. Dash®

National Honey Board

National Pork Board

Nestlé USA

New York Apple Association, Inc.

The Quaker® Oatmeal Kitchens

Reckitt Benckiser Inc.

Sargento® Foods Inc.

The J.M. Smucker Company

StarKist Seafood Company

The Sugar Association, Inc.

Sun•Maid® Growers of California

Reprinted with permission of Sunkist Growers, Inc.

Texas Peanut Producers Board

Unilever Bestfoods North America

USA Rice

Veg•All®

Metric Chart

VOLUME MEASUREMENTS (dry)

$^1/_8$ teaspoon = 0.5 mL
$^1/_4$ teaspoon = 1 mL
$^1/_2$ teaspoon = 2 mL
$^3/_4$ teaspoon = 4 mL
1 teaspoon = 5 mL
1 tablespoon = 15 mL
2 tablespoons = 30 mL
$^1/_4$ cup = 60 mL
$^1/_3$ cup = 75 mL
$^1/_2$ cup = 125 mL
$^2/_3$ cup = 150 mL
$^3/_4$ cup = 175 mL
1 cup = 250 mL
2 cups = 1 pint = 500 mL
3 cups = 750 mL
4 cups = 1 quart = 1 L

VOLUME MEASUREMENTS (fluid)

1 fluid ounce (2 tablespoons) = 30 mL
4 fluid ounces ($^1/_2$ cup) = 125 mL
8 fluid ounces (1 cup) = 250 mL
12 fluid ounces (1$^1/_2$ cups) = 375 mL
16 fluid ounces (2 cups) = 500 mL

WEIGHTS (mass)

$^1/_2$ ounce = 15 g
1 ounce = 30 g
3 ounces = 90 g
4 ounces = 120 g
8 ounces = 225 g
10 ounces = 285 g
12 ounces = 360 g
16 ounces = 1 pound = 450 g

DIMENSIONS

$^1/_{16}$ inch = 2 mm
$^1/_8$ inch = 3 mm
$^1/_4$ inch = 6 mm
$^1/_2$ inch = 1.5 cm
$^3/_4$ inch = 2 cm
1 inch = 2.5 cm

OVEN TEMPERATURES

250°F = 120°C
275°F = 140°C
300°F = 150°C
325°F = 160°C
350°F = 180°C
375°F = 190°C
400°F = 200°C
425°F = 220°C
450°F = 230°C

BAKING PAN SIZES

Utensil	Size in Inches/Quarts	Metric Volume	Size in Centimeters
Baking or Cake Pan (square or rectangular)	8×8×2	2 L	20×20×5
	9×9×2	2.5 L	23×23×5
	12×8×2	3 L	30×20×5
	13×9×2	3.5 L	33×23×5
Loaf Pan	8×4×3	1.5 L	20×10×7
	9×5×3	2 L	23×13×7
Round Layer Cake Pan	8×1½	1.2 L	20×4
	9×1½	1.5 L	23×4
Pie Plate	8×1¼	750 mL	20×3
	9×1¼	1 L	23×3
Baking Dish or Casserole	1 quart	1 L	—
	1½ quart	1.5 L	—
	2 quart	2 L	—